TRIO
WRITING 3

The Intersection of
Vocabulary, Grammar, & Writing

Alice Savage & Colin Ward

OXFORD

UNIVERSITY PRESS

198 Madison Avenue
New York, NY 10016 USA

Great Clarendon Street, Oxford, ox2 6dp, United Kingdom

Oxford University Press is a department of the University of Oxford.
It furthers the University's objective of excellence in research, scholarship,
and education by publishing worldwide. Oxford is a registered trade
mark of Oxford University Press in the UK and in certain other countries

Adult Content Director: Stephanie Karras

Publisher: Sharon Sargent

Managing Editor: Tracey Gibbins

Senior Development Editor: Anna Norris

Head of Digital, Design, and Production: Bridget O'Lavin

Executive Art and Design Manager: Maj-Britt Hagsted

Content Production Manager: Julie Armstrong

Design Project Manager: Lisa Donovan

Image Manager: Trisha Masterson

Senior Image Editor: Fran Newman

Production Coordinator: Christopher Espejo

ISBN: 978 0 19 485421 4 Student Book 3 with Online Practice Pack
ISBN: 978 0 19 485422 1 Student Book 3 as pack component
ISBN: 978 0 19 485423 8 Online Practice website

Printed in China

This book is printed on paper from certified and well-managed sources

ACKNOWLEDGEMENTS

Cover Design: Yin Ling Wong

Illustrations by: Ben Hasler, pg. 36–37, 74–75, 112–113; Joseph Taylor, pg. 14, 20–21,
58–59, 96–97; 5W Infographics, pg. 17, 74, 54, 128.

*We would also like to thank the following for permission to reproduce the following
photographs:* pg. 1: Mark Daffey/Getty Images, ArtPix / Alamyx/Alamy, John
W. Banagan/Getty Images; pg. 2: Transtock/Corbis; pg. 19: Krafft Angerer/
Getty Images, Ariel Skelley/Getty Images, Dusit/Shutterstock; pg. 23: auremar/
Shutterstock, Don Mason/Blend Images/Corbis, Agencja Fotograficzna Caro/
Alamy, Lena Ivanova/Shutterstock, Nullplus/Getty Images, supergenijalac/
Shutterstock; pg. 39: WENN Ltd/Alamy, B Christopher/Alamy, g-stockstudio/
Shutterstock, DK Limited/Corbis, Andersen Ross/ Agefotostock, Dreamframer/
Shutterstock; pg. 40: Blend Images/Alamy, Dora Zett/Shutterstock; pg. 45: OUP/
Photodisc, Iakov Filimonov/Shutterstock, Blend Images/Alamy; pg. 47: Paul
Thompsom/Getty Images, DNY59/iStock, Charles Silvey/Getty Images, Elyse
Lewin/Getty Images; pg. 57: Filip Fuxa/Shutterstock, Sailorr/Shutterstock,
dieKleinert/Alamy; pg. 61: Georgia Court/Getty Images, Image Source/Getty
Images, Aron Hsiao/Shutterstock, fotoVoyager/iStock, Alaska Stock/Alamy, Gary K
Smith/Loop Images/Corbis; pg. 70: SNEHIT/Shutterstock; pg. 72: FRANS LANTING,
MINT IMAGES / SCIENCE PHOTO LIBRARY; pg. 75: Alan Gignoux/Alamy, Maynard
Owen Williams/National Geographic Society/Corbis; pg. 77: keith morris/
Alamy, Robert Harding World Imagery/Alamy, Macduff Everton/Corbis, Nickolay
Vinokurov/Shutterstock, tormentor3/iStock, FloridaStock/Shutterstock; pg. 86:
Vaclav Volrab/Shutterstock, IM_photo/Shutterstock; pg. 90: denisgo/Shutterstock,
Esteban De Armas/Shutterstock; pg. 95: Gerry Angus/Icon Sportswire/Corbis,
OLIVER BERG/epa/Corbis, Ian Shaw/Alamy; pg. 99: zixia/Alamy, Pali Rao/Getty
Images, GoGo Images Corporation/Alamy, Jon Feingersh/Blend Images/Corbis,
Wavebreak Media Ltd./Corbis, clayton addison/NewSport/Corbis; pg. 115:
Francesco Tremolada/SOPA RF/SOPA/Corbis, Ariel Skelley/Blend Images/Corbis,
Kord.com/Agefotostock, Michael Hevesy/Corbis, altafulla/Shutterstock, Bartco/
Getty Images; pg. 116: Agencja Fotograficzna Caro/Alamy; pg. 117: Thinkstock
Images/Getty Images, ALESSANDRO DELLA BELLA/Keystone/Corbis; pg. 122:
Nata-Lia/Shutterstock.

REVIEWERS

We would like to acknowledge the following individuals for their input during the development of the series:

Aubrey Adrianson
Ferris State University
U.S.A.

Sedat Akayoğlu
Middle East Technical University
Turkey

Lisa Alton
University of Alberta
Canada

Türkan Aydin
Çanakkale Onsekiz Mart University
Turkey

Pelin Tekinalp Cakmak
Marmara University, School of Foreign Languages
Turkey

Karen E. Caldwell
Zayed University
U.A.E.

Danielle Chircop
Kaplan International English
U.S.A.

Jennifer Chung
Gwangju ECC
South Korea

Elaine Cockerham
Higher College of Technology
Oman

Abdullah Coskun
Abant Izzet Baysal University
Turkey

Linda Crocker
University of Kentucky
U.S.A.

Adem Onur Fedai
Fatih University Preparatory School
Turkey

Greg Holloway
Kyushu Institute of Technology
Japan

Elizabeth Houtrow
Soongsil University
South Korea

Shu-Chen Huang
National Chengchi University
Taipei City

Ece Selva Küçükoğlu
METU School of Foreign Languages
Turkey

Margaret Martin
Xavier University
U.S.A.

Murray McMahon
University of Alberta
Canada

Shaker Ali Mohammed Al-Mohammadi
Buraimi University College
Oman

Eileen O'Brien
Khalifa University of Science, Technology and Research
U.A.E.

Fernanda Ortiz
Center for English as a Second Language at University of Arizona
U.S.A.

Ebru Osborne
Yildiz Technical University
Turkey

Joshua Pangborn
Kaplan International
U.S.A.

Erkan Kadir Şimşek
Akdeniz University Manavgat Vocational College
Turkey

Veronica Struck
Sussex County Community College
U.S.A.

Clair Taylor
Gifu Shotoku Gakuen University
Japan

Melody Traylor
Higher Colleges of Technology
U.A.E.

Sabiha Tunc
Baskent University English Language Department
Turkey

John Vogels
Dubai Men's College
U.A.E.

Author Acknowledgments

We would like to thank the many people who were involved in the development of *Trio Writing*, which began over Mexican food in Houston, where the idea for it was born in a meeting with Sharon Sargent, our friend and guide throughout this long process. Sharon, thank you for believing in us.

We are indebted to our brilliant editorial team: Tracey Gibbins, Mariel DeKranis, Keyana Shaw, Karin Kipp, and Anita Raducanu. We'd also like to give a special thanks to Stephanie Karras, who has been instrumental in bringing the idea to fruition.

Finally, we'd like to thank our friends and families, Margi Wald for sharing ideas and resources, our spouses Stefanie and Masoud who good-naturedly endured the endless beep of text messages as we sent ideas back and forth, and our children who made their own snacks when we were on a roll. It has been a wonderful journey, and we are very grateful to have had such fantastic fellow travelers.

—A. S. and C. W.

CONTENTS

UNIT 2 Science *(continued)*

CHAPTER	ACADEMIC CONTENT	LANGUAGE FOCUS	CRITICAL THINKING
6 Responding to Art page 90	Art that shows future transportation solutions	*would* and *would be able to*	Making predictions and imagining solutions

UNIT WRAP UP Extend Your Skills page 94

UNIT 3 Media Studies pages 95–132

CHAPTER	▲ VOCABULARY	▲▲ GRAMMAR	▲▲▲ WRITING
7 How Can Celebrities Influence People? page 96	Oxford 2000 🔑 words to talk about people in the news	*which* and *which means that* *even though* and *even when*	Writing an essay about effects Referring to the names of people and organizations
8 What Is an Issue in the News? page 112	Oxford 2000 🔑 words to talk about issues in the news	Adjective clauses with *where* *if* to talk about possibility	Writing a summary and a personal response *on the other hand*
	ACADEMIC CONTENT	LANGUAGE FOCUS	CRITICAL THINKING
9 Applying Information from a Bar Graph page 128	A bar graph showing social media behavior	Reporting percentages	Evaluating information

UNIT WRAP UP Extend Your Skills page 132

The Oxford 2000 🔑
List of Keywords

Welcome to Trio Writing

Building Better Writers...From the Beginning

Trio Writing includes three levels of Student Books, Online Practice, and Teacher Support.

Level 1/CEFR A1

Level 2/CEFR A2

Level 3/CEFR B1

Essential Digital Content

iTools USB with Classroom Resources

Trio Writing weaves together contextualized vocabulary words, grammar skills, and writing strategies to provide students with the tools they need for successful academic writing at the earliest stages of language acquisition.

Vocabulary Based On the Oxford 2000 🔑 Keywords

Trio Writing's vocabulary is based on the 2,000 most important and useful words to learn at the early stages of language learning, making content approachable for low-level learners.

Explicit, Contextualized Skills Instruction

Contextualized Grammar Notes and Writing Strategies are presented to teach the most useful and relevant skills students need to achieve success in their writing.

Readiness Unit

For added flexibility, each level of *Trio Writing* begins with an optional Readiness Unit to provide fundamental English tools for beginning students.

INSIDE EACH UNIT

▲ VOCABULARY

Theme-based chapters set a context for learning.

Essential, explicit skills help beginning learners to generate independent academic writing.

CHAPTER **4**

When Did Nature Amaze You?

- Use the past perfect with *so* and *because*
- Use quoted speech
- Introduce a narrative essay
- Use time markers
- Write a narrative essay about an experience in nature

▲ VOCABULARY ▶ Oxford 2000 ✎ words to talk about experiences in nature

A. Write the letter of each group of sentences above the correct picture. Circle the boldfaced words you know. Discuss the words with a partner. Use a dictionary to help you with new words.

a.
The lake was **calm** because there was no wind.
A group of birds was **flying through the air**.

b.
Waves on the river **were crashing into** our boat.
We came to a powerful **waterfall**.

c.
We had **an amazing view** because we saw hundreds of **stars**.
The stars were **shining brightly** in the night sky.

d.
A **thunderstorm** with dark, gray clouds **appeared in the distance**.
Flashes of lightning hit the ground.

e.
My friends and I **reached the top** of the mountain.
It was cold because the sun **had disappeared behind** the clouds.

f.
We stood under a bridge to **escape the heavy rain**.
We waited there for the **rough** weather to pass.

3. _____

4. _____

5. _____

6. _____

1. _____

2. _____

B. Ask and answer each question with a partner. Try to use the target vocabulary.

1. What places in nature make you feel **calm** and peaceful?
2. What can make the **stars disappear** at night?
3. When did you see an **amazing** sunset?
4. How do you know when a **thunderstorm** is close to you?
5. When was the last time you experienced **heavy rain**?

Oxford 2000 ✎
Use the Oxford 2000 list on page 133 to find more words to describe the pictures on these pages. Share your words with a partner.

58   Unit 2 | Chapter 4

Vocabulary   59

Vocabulary focuses on the Oxford 2000 list of keywords and is introduced in context to help students internalize meaning.

Four pages of vocabulary instruction and activities give students new ways to use the words they learn.

▲▲ GRAMMAR

A two-part grammar presentation with writing practice recycles key vocabulary.

Achievable writing models provide examples of grammar skills in the context of each chapter's writing assignment.

▲▲ GRAMMAR
▶ Past perfect with *so* and *because*
▶ Quoted speech

A. Read Sara's essay. How old do you think Sara was? Why?

Starry Night

One winter, my family was traveling to a small town in the mountains. The sun had already set, so the roads were dark. I was sleeping in the car when a cold wind woke me up. My father was standing outside the car in the dark. "Come out, Sara," he said. "I want to show you something."

My father helped me out of the car. Then he pointed at the sky. Hundreds of stars were shining brightly. They were beautiful colors and different sizes. Some of them were close together in bright groups, and others were far apart. Suddenly, I saw one star fly across the sky. I tried to follow it with my eyes, but it had already disappeared into the darkness.

I was amazed because I had never seen the night sky so clearly. The stars were bright because we were far from the city and the air was clear. Later, I thought about the great distance to the stars and the power of nature. It was a beautiful experience, and I will never forget it.

B. Read the sentences about the essay in Activity A. Number the events in the correct order.

____ a. Sara's father pointed to the stars in the sky.

____ b. Sara thought about the distance to the stars.

____ c. Sara's family started driving to the mountains.

____ d. A star disappeared into the darkness.

____ e. Sara fell asleep in the car.

Grammar Note

Past perfect with *so* and *because*
The past perfect tense shows that one action was completed before a second action. Writers often use the past perfect tense with *so* and *because* to explain a reason.

    reason
The sun had already set, **so** the roads were dark.

        reason
We went inside **because** it had begun to rain.

The past perfect uses *had (not)* + past participle.
We were tired because we had hiked a long way.
The sun had not set, so we had time to get back home.

C. Complete the sentences with the past perfect tense verbs in the box.

had become	had forgotten
had blown	had had
had changed	had heard
had disappeared	had hit

1. The sky _had become_ dark, so we decided to go inside.

2. We _____ to bring food, so we were hungry.

3. The trees were black because lightning _____ them.

4. We were worried because we _____ thunder.

5. The sun _____ behind the clouds, so the air felt cooler.

6. Our view of the forest _____ because we were higher in the mountains.

7. I was happy because we _____ an amazing time.

8. We were surprised because the wind _____ open our kitchen window.

GO ONLINE for more practice

Trio Writing Online Practice extends learning beyond the classroom, providing students with additional practice and support for each chapter's vocabulary, grammar, and writing instruction.

D. Complete each sentence with the verb in parentheses. Use *had (not)* + the past participle form of the verb.

1. (got) It was easier to see because the sky _had gotten_ brighter.

2. (appear) We were worried because dark clouds _____ in the distance.

3. (be) I _____ to the top of the mountain before, so I did not know what to expect.

4. (come) Winter _____, so the days were cold and gray.

5. (change) The trees were orange and red because the leaves _____ color.

6. (bring) We were lost because we _____ a map with us.

Grammar Note

Quoted speech
Writers use quoted speech to write the exact words people said. Use quotation marks (" ") to begin and end a quote. Capitalize the first letter of the quote, and put punctuation inside the quotation mark.

    "Please be careful."   "Look at that!"
                "Was that thunder?"

Writers often follow a quote with a subject and a reporting verb such as *said*, *asked*, or *shouted*. The punctuation before the end of the quote is different for each reporting verb.

comma (,)	"Please be careful," my parents **said**.
	"I think it's going to be a beautiful day," I **said**.
question mark (?)	"Was that thunder?" my brother **asked**.
	"Are you tired?" I **asked**.
exclamation point (!)	"Look at that!" he **shouted**.
	"There's something in those bushes!" my friend **shouted**.

When writers separate a quote with a reporting verb, the second quote begins a new sentence.

                    new sentence
"Come out, Sara," he said. "I want to show you something."

GO ONLINE for more practice

Each grammar lesson contains two Grammar Notes, which are matched closely to the writing task for supportive grammar instruction.

E. Read the sentences. Add quotation marks and correct punctuation.

1. Let's go home. my friend said.

2. I'm not worried I said.

3. What time is it I asked.

4. Watch out my brother shouted.

5. Do you want to keep going I asked.

6. It's getting dark I said. Let's stop here.

F. Write sentences with the words in parentheses. Use quoted speech and correct punctuation.

1. A flash of lightning lit the sky.
"That was close!" my friend shouted. "Let's go!"
(that was close / my friend shouted / let's go)

2. I was pointing to the star, but my son couldn't find it.
_____
(Look closer / I said)

3. _____
(are you ready / my father asked)
I smiled nervously and stepped into the boat.

4. We were walking through the forest when I heard a strange noise.
_____
(did you hear that / I asked)

5. _____
(I think we'll be fine / my friend said)
I was not sure because the rain was not stopping.

6. My friend was getting too close to the dog.
_____
(stop / I shouted / he doesn't look friendly)

Chant
GO ONLINE for the Chapter 4 Vocabulary & Grammar Chant

Vocabulary and Grammar Chants found online help students internalize the target grammar structure and vocabulary for greater accuracy and fluency when writing.

▲▲▲ WRITING

Trio Writing guides students to write essays using models and scaffolded tasks.

The Writing lesson builds on the first two lessons by bringing the language and theme together in a six-step, scaffolded writing task. Even the earliest-level language learners are able to create a portfolio of academic writing with *Trio Writing*.

▲▲▲ **WRITING** ► Introducing a narrative essay
► Past time markers

Writing Assignment
A narrative essay about an experience in nature

Nature can be powerful and unexpected. In this assignment, you will write a narrative essay about an experience in nature that had a powerful effect on you.

1. In the **introduction**, give the setting. When did it happen? Where were you? Who were you with? Include other details about the setting that are important.

2. In the **support paragraph(s)**, describe the experience. In this part, focus on nature, not your feelings. Try to describe it fully by including as many details as you can. What did you see? What did you hear? What happened?

3. In the **conclusion**, explain how the experience made you feel. What did you learn from the experience about yourself or the natural world?

Step 1 PREPARE

A. Read Khiem's narrative essay. How did his experience change his view of the Pacuare River?

On the Pacuare River

One summer, my friends and I decided to take a trip to the Pacuare River in Costa Rica. We got to the river early in the morning. I was excited because I had never tried river rafting, and I didn't know what to expect.

We got in the boat and started rafting. Eventually, we heard rough water ahead of us. "Get ready!" my friend shouted. All of a sudden, the water moved quickly, and powerful waves crashed into our boat. "Look at that!" my friend Sam said. He was pointing to a high waterfall in the distance. At first, it was quiet, but when we reached it, we heard its powerful crash.

It is hard to describe the Pacuare River. In photos, it looks green and calm, but rafting made me view it differently. Now I appreciate its true power, and my friends and I can't wait to go back and experience its dangerous beauty again.

66   Unit 2 | Chapter 4

B. Read the summary sentences for the paragraphs in the essay in Activity A. Then number them in the same order as the essay.

_____ a. Rafting made Khiem appreciate the river's power.

_____ b. Khiem and his friends made plans to go river rafting in Costa Rica.

_____ c. Strong water carried their boat down the river to a waterfall.

Writing Strategy

Introducing a narrative essay

A narrative essay describes an experience using details and observations. The introduction often tells the background setting or the time and place of the event. Time phrases such as *one winter, one year,* and *one day* can introduce the setting.

The thesis statement prepares readers for the action of the story. It makes readers curious about a problem or an unexpected situation but doesn't tell about the main event.

Examples:

I was excited because I had never tried river rafting, and I did not know what to expect.

"Come out, Sara," my father said. "I want to show you something."

C. Use a phrase from the box to introduce the setting of each introduction. Underline the detail(s) that help describe the setting.

| One evening | One morning | One summer | One winter |

1. *One summer*, my family and I took a vacation to the California coast. The days were hot, but the air was clean, and the ocean smelled beautiful.

2. _____, I was riding my motorcycle to work. It had rained hard the night before, so the streets were wet. There were still some clouds in the sky.

3. _____, my friends and I decided to go skiing in the mountains. The weather was cold, and there was fresh snow on the ground. We stood at the top of the mountain and looked down.

4. _____, I was sitting on my front porch. I had already eaten dinner, and I was enjoying the view of the sunset and the pink clouds in the sky.

Multiple Writing Strategies are embedded within the Writing Process to present focused instruction that supports the assignment. Writing Strategies feature additional language points and writing skills so that students become aware of the structure of academic writing.

Step 5 EDIT

A. Read the essay. Find and correct nine mistakes. The first mistake is corrected for you.

Orange and Black

    comma
One winter. my family and I took a trip to a forest in northern Mexico. It still a little dark because we had got up early. "Where are they" my daughter asked.

Eventually we heard them. We looked up, and hundreds of Monarch butterflies were flying through the air. "Look at the trees" my daughter shouted, "They're orange and black!" We stood in amazement because we never seen so many butterflies before. The trees were covered in their beautiful colors, and the forest looked like a painting.

Seeing the Monarch butterflies was an amaze experience. I saw the power of nature, and my daughter saw all of its beauty. It was a special moment that my family and I will never forget.

The Writing Assignment icon highlights scaffolded steps in the writing process.

B. Read your essay again. Check (✓) the things in your essay.

Editing Checklist

○ 1. Capital letters, periods, and commas

○ 2. Past perfect with *so* and *because*

○ 3. Quoted speech

○ 4. Past time markers (e.g., *suddenly, eventually, still*)

C. Now write your final essay. Use the Editing Checklist to help you.

Step 6 PUBLISH

Follow these steps to publish your essay.

Publishing Steps

• Share your paragraphs with a partner.

• Answer the questions.

    • What details make the narrative interesting to read?

    • Have you had a similar experience in nature? When?

• Put your essay in your portfolio!

Critical Thinking Question

What can nature give people? Name three things.

Critical Thinking Questions provide further opportunities to reflect on the topic of the writing task.

72   Unit 2 | Chapter 4

Writing   73

Academic Content Writing Task

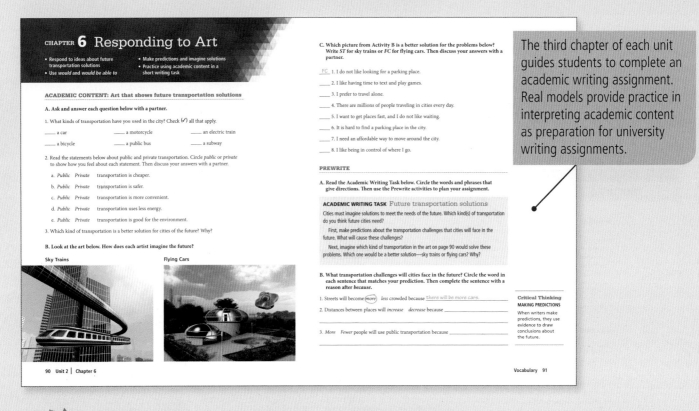

The third chapter of each unit guides students to complete an academic writing assignment. Real models provide practice in interpreting academic content as preparation for university writing assignments.

Trio Writing Online Practice: Essential Digital Content

With content that is exclusive to the digital experience, *Trio Writing* Online Practice provides multiple opportunities for skills practice and acquisition—beyond the classroom and beyond the page.

Each unit of *Trio Writing* is accompanied by a variety of automatically graded activities. Students' progress is recorded, tracked, and fed back to the instructor.

Grammar and Vocabulary Chants help students internalize the target grammar structure and vocabulary for greater accuracy and fluency when writing.

Vocabulary and Grammar Chants provide further accuracy and fluency practice for every chapter.

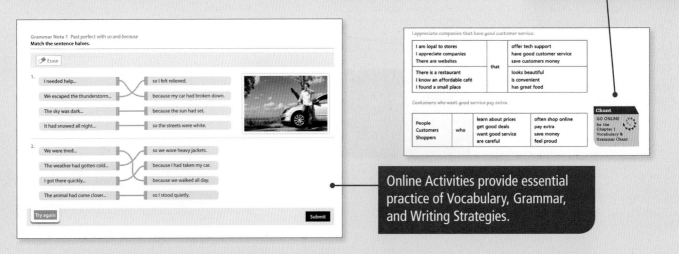

Online Activities provide essential practice of Vocabulary, Grammar, and Writing Strategies.

Use the access code on the inside front cover to log in at **www.oxfordlearn.com/login**.
Need help? Watch a tutorial video at **www.oxfordlearn.com/howtoregister**.

Readiness Unit

Words and Phrases

Word forms
Academic words
Phrases

Clauses and Sentences

Simple sentences
Sentences with gerunds and infinitives
Compound sentences
Compound sentences with transitions
Complex sentences

Paragraphs and Essays

Paragraphs
Essays
Academic writing assignments
Writing from content

UNIT WRAP UP Extend Your Skills

▲ WORDS AND PHRASES

Word Forms

Many words can be used in different ways. The forms usually change, but not always.

Adjective	Noun	Verb	Adverb
beautiful	beauty		beautifully
dangerous	danger	endanger	dangerously
	exploration	explore	
	motorcycle		
powerful	power	power	powerfully

A. Use the chart above to answer the questions.

1. What type of word usually has *-ly* at the end? _____

2. Which word has the same form as a noun and verb? _____

3. Which words have four forms? _____

4. Which verb adds *en-* to the noun form? _____

5. Which word has only one form? _____

B. Check (✓) the phrases that describe the picture.

_____✓___ 1. a beautiful mountain road

_____ 2. a powerful motorcycle

_____ 3. explore the beach

_____ 4. drive dangerously in the city

_____ 5. the beauty of nature

Academic Words

Many words in academic writing have similar meanings to regular words.

Regular word	Academic word	Meaning
see	*observe*	see and notice details
have	*include*	group things that are part of something
help	*benefit*	have a positive effect on someone or something
show	*suggest*	say that something is good advice or that the writer thinks is true
cannot happen *can happen*	*impossible* *possible*	something that cannot be real something that can be real
make	*develop*	to make something bigger or more important by adding new things or ideas

A. Use the chart to fill in the blank in each question below. Then ask and answer the questions with a partner.

Adjective	Noun	Verb
beneficial	*benefit*	*benefit*
	development	*develop*
observable	*observation/observer*	*observe*
	suggestion	*suggest*

1. What _____observations_____ do you have about how weather affects people?

2. What does a smile _____ when you meet a new person?

3. How can your city _____ safer neighborhoods?

4. What are two _____ of speaking another language?

5. How do intelligent people _____ skills for a career?

6. The last time you went to a restaurant, what did you _____ about the service?

7. How can your success _____ your family?

B. Check (✓) the sentences that are true about you.

_____ 1. I like to share **observations** of people and places with a partner.

_____ 2. I am **developing** new techniques for learning vocabulary.

_____ 3. My book **includes** online activities.

_____ 4. I often **suggest** ideas during group work.

_____ 5. I usually think about different **possibilities** before I make a decision.

_____ 6. I believe there are **benefits** to traveling to different countries.

_____ 7. When people give me **suggestions** about my work, I think about them carefully.

_____ 8. I am a good **observer** because I remember the things I see and experience.

Phrases

In English, words combine with other words to form phrases.

Adjectives with nouns	Verbs with nouns	Verbs with adverbs
a famous artist	develop a city	act differently
a local community	affect society	talk politely
a successful career	save energy	walk slowly
a powerful person	have money	think carefully
a dangerous place	explore a forest	work quickly
a difficult task	discuss an idea	see clearly

Write three more phrases for each column by combining the words from the chart above in new ways. Make sure the new phrases have meaning.

Adjectives with nouns	Verbs with nouns	Verbs with adverbs
a local artist	discuss society	act quickly

▲▲ CLAUSES AND SENTENCES

Simple Sentences

Words and phrases work together to form clauses. A clause has a subject and verb. Sentences that have one clause are simple sentences. There are three common types of simple sentences.

A	B	C
one subject/one verb	two subjects/one verb	one subject/two verbs
Workers discuss problems. The government achieved its goal.	Parks and sidewalks improved the city. My classmates and I take the bus.	Travelers stay in hotels and shop in markets. He saved money and went to Paris.

A. Read each simple sentence, and write A, B, or C from the chart above to identify its type.

_____A_____ 1. I hope to design software for a company.

_____ 2. The community faced a challenge.

_____ 3. She painted pictures and wrote stories.

_____ 4. Motorcycles and bicycles save energy.

_____ 5. My family and I lived in a building downtown.

_____ 6. The storm got worse and slowed traffic.

B. Add subjects and verbs to complete the chart with different types of sentences.

one subject/one verb	two subjects/one verb	one subject/two verbs
My friend texts.	My friend and her sister text.	My friend texts and walks.
	Students and workers read books.	
My brothers eat spicy food.		
		Friends laugh and talk.

Gerunds and infinitives help writers describe actions, but they do not show time.

Gerunds are verb + *ing* and are frequently used in these ways.	
As a subject	*Writing* a book takes a long time.
As the object of a few verbs	*She enjoys shopping.*
As the object of a preposition	*They talked about working together.*

Infinitives are *to* + verb and are frequently used in these ways.	
After many verbs	*Travelers want to see beautiful places.*
After many objects	*People expected him to quit.*
To give a purpose	*They bought vegetables to make soup.*
With *it is* + adjective	*It is important to wear comfortable shoes.* *It is difficult for students to work.*

A. Complete each sentence by circling the correct form of the word.

1. People need   *to work*   *working*   so they can pay their rent.

2. Nowadays, many people use computers   *to do*   *doing*   their jobs.

3. It is important   *to keep*   *keeping*   parks clean so other people can enjoy them.

4. Many people are interested in   *to learn*   *learning*   another language.

5. My friend Alice is active, and she enjoys   *to swim*   *swimming*.

6. It is beneficial   *to get*   *getting*   eight hours of sleep every night.

B. Use the following gerunds to describe your opinion about each activity.

playing soccer	studying	eating in restaurants
cooking	traveling	exercising

1. *Eating in restaurants is expensive but fun.*
2. _____
3. _____
4. _____
5. _____
6. _____

C. Use the following verb infinitive combinations to describe future plans.

hope to see	want to understand	have to learn
plan to work	would like to find	

1. *I hope to see Paris in the future.*
2. _____
3. _____
4. _____
5. _____

Compound Sentences

Two clauses can be joined with a comma and *and*, *but*, *so*, or *or* to form a compound sentence.

Use *and* to connect similar ideas.	*Families gather in the park, **and** the children play games.*
Use *but* to show a difference.	*Some people take off their shoes at the door, **but** other people do not.*
Use *so* to explain a result.	*The new neighbors were friendly, **so** we invited them for dinner.*
Use *or* to show there is more than one possibility or choice.	*Most hotel guests are tourists, **or** they have come for business.*

Choose the best clause to complete each compound sentence.

1. Teenagers prefer to communicate by text, but

    a. they like phone calls.   b. their parents usually make phone calls.

2. Doctors have a lot of responsibility, so

    a. they work carefully.   b. they do not solve problems.

3. I study engineering, but

    a. I had a successful career.   b. my brother studies photography.

4. People take the train, or

    a. they ride the bus.   b. it saves time and energy.

5. Buildings in my neighborhood are old, but

    a. they are crowded.   b. they are beautiful.

6. The government built a stadium far from the city center, so

    a. people complained.   b. sports events were downtown.

Compound Sentences with Transitions

Transitions signal relationships among ideas. Sentences with transitions are compound sentences, but they have different punctuation. The first clause ends with a semicolon, and there is a comma after the transition word(s).

semicolon   comma

The builders faced many difficult challenges; **however,** *the engineers found solutions.*

Commonly used transitions		
Transition	**Purpose**	**Example with a semicolon to join clauses**
in addition *also*	to add information	*He wrote books about his travels;* **in addition,** *he made short movies about the people in different countries.*
however	to signal a contrast	*The storm was dangerous;* **however,** *the travelers did not want to stop.*
consequently *as a result*	to show a result	*Many people like to learn about the lives of movie actors;* **as a result,** *media photographers follow actors everywhere.*
in fact *interestingly*	to add supporting facts	*Teenagers like to shop in stores;* **in fact,** *78% of girls and 75% of boys prefer stores to online shopping.*

Read each sentence. Then write a transition to complete the idea. More than one transition may be correct. Use correct punctuation.

1. The train was fast; as a result, _____ passengers arrived early.

2. The hotel was beautiful_____ guests complained about the service.

3. Many people ride their bicycles to work_____ they get exercise every day.

4. Tourists enjoy exploring the old neighborhoods; _____ they can take a tour on a river boat.

5. The city has built a bridge across the street_____ people have a way to cross safely.

6. People benefit from nature_____ doctors suggest that being in nature improves health.

Complex Sentences

A complex sentence has a main clause and a dependent clause. The dependent clause has a subordinating conjunction such as *when, while, before, after,* or *because.*

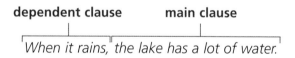

dependent clause	main clause

When it rains, *the lake has a lot of water.*

A dependent clause at the beginning of a sentence introduces information before the main clause.	***When*** <u>we moved</u>, we had to say goodbye to our friends. ***While*** <u>we were driving</u>, we played word games.
A dependent clause at the end of a sentence adds information after the main clause.	She got a job at a hotel ***after*** <u>she graduated</u>. He became famous ***because*** <u>he had talent</u>.

A. Write a subordinating conjunction from the box to complete each sentence. Add punctuation where necessary. Some conjunctions may be used more than once.

after	because	before	when	while

1. _____While_____ we were in Italy, we visited historic buildings.

2. _____ we went to Italy we saved money and made careful plans.

3. _____ we came home we shared pictures and stories with our friends.

4. We want to go back _____ we had a good time.

5. We did not know a lot about Italy _____ we went there.

6. We took a lot of photographs _____ we were traveling.

7. We started to eat in parks _____ the weather became nice.

8. It was important to visit relatives _____ we came home from our trip.

B. Use the words in the charts to write complex sentences. Use correct punctuation.

When they were looking at the view, the guests were happy.

After	they arrived	the restaurant served dinner
Before	they saw the view	people talked about the news
When	they were eating	many travelers took pictures
While	they were looking at the view	the parks became crowded
	the sun went down	the guests were happy

Ansel Adams became famous because he took beautiful pictures of nature.

Ansel Adams became famous		his parents did not expect it
Cho was a successful athlete	because	he took beautiful pictures of nature
Gabriel made a lot of money last year	even though	there were challenges
		he worked hard

Paragraphs

A paragraph develops an idea with a topic sentence and supporting facts, explanations and observations. When a writer shifts focus to a new or related idea, the writer starts a new paragraph.

topic sentence —

<u>Vietnam is a country of rivers, and these rivers are important to its people.</u> Farmers depend on many rivers to grow food. Other rivers provide power to cities. Some of the more beautiful rivers are important for tourism.

support sentences

indent 5 spaces

topic sentence changes the focus from an overview of Vietnamese rivers to focus on one river

The Mekong River is so big and so important that it is world famous as a symbol of Vietnam. Local farmers depend on the Mekong for fresh water and nutrients that they need to grow rice and feed the country. In fact, the Mekong River Delta is called the Rice Bowl because farmers there grow most of the country's rice. They also use the water to grow fruit trees and vegetables.

A. Read each paragraph below. Underline the topic sentence. Write the number of support sentences.

_____ 1.   Medicine offers excellent career opportunities. There are many jobs to choose from, and people can decide on the career that is right for them. Also, many medical jobs pay well. In fact, doctors are some of the highest-paid professionals. In addition, people who practice medicine help other people. They feel good about their work.

_____ 2.   Sugar affects students' attention. A little sugar can be good for learning. Some students do better on tests after they eat a small piece of candy or chocolate. However, experts recommend a small amount. A lot of sugar is not better.

B. Check (✓) the box with effective paragraphing to show a shift in focus. Explain your choice to a partner.

☐ Many travelers like to visit zoos to see animals from different countries. Usually the animals are separated from people and each other, but a zoo in Denmark is changing the rules.

Zootopia will be different in several ways. First, it will not have lonely animals. The animals that are social will be together. Second, the builders will hide all the walls, so people and animals will not feel separated. Third, people will use a variety of transportation methods to move through the zoo.

☐ Many travelers like to visit zoos to see animals from different countries.

Usually the animals are separated from people and each other, but a zoo in Denmark is changing the rules. Zootopia will be different in several ways. First, it will not have lonely animals.

The animals that are social will be together. Second, the builders will hide all the walls, so people and animals will not feel separated. People will use a variety of transportation methods to move through the zoo.

C. Match the number of each topic sentence to a vacation picture. Then write two or three supporting details for each paragraph. Use your imagination.

☐  ☐  ☐

1. We ate breakfast at an outdoor café. _____

_____

2. We took a boat ride on the river. _____

_____

3. We went shopping at a famous store. _____

_____

The goal of an academic essay is to learn about a topic and then explain the learning in writing. This requires critical thinking. To think critically, writers look at information, make connections between ideas, and develop new knowledge about a topic.

Most essays have three main parts, and each part has one or more paragraphs.

How GPS Changed the World

The **introduction** provides background and helps the reader understand the focus of the essay. This focus, or **thesis statement**, usually comes at the end of the introduction.

Cell phone technology and the Internet have changed life in many ways. In order to understand these changes, it is helpful to compare life for drivers before and after the Global Positioning System (GPS) was invented.

The **support paragraphs** develop the thesis with facts, examples, and observations that show learning and thinking. Writers can include one, two, or several support paragraphs.

In the past, drivers did not know the fastest way to get to new places. They had to use a map, and they stopped at stores to ask for directions. It was not easy; however, people learned a lot about their cities because they had to learn their way around.

Now, people put an address in their GPS, and they can choose a route. The GPS tells them about traffic and the best way to go. The GPS shows them new streets, and they do not get lost. Sometimes the GPS loses the signal, or it gives wrong information; however, drivers with a GPS usually feel more confident than drivers without one.

The **conclusion** allows the writer to comment on what the information means. One or more conclusion paragraphs might give an opinion, advice, or prediction that relates to the thesis statement.

A GPS offers many benefits for drivers who plan to visit a new restaurant or city. They do not have to worry about getting lost; in addition, they feel comfortable knowing the time and distance of the trip. When the GPS does not work, they can still ask for directions. As a result, GPS has given drivers a lot of freedom that they did not have before.

A. Read *How GPS Changed the World* again, and answer the questions. Discuss your answers with a partner.

1. Do you use a GPS? Does your experience match the writer's analysis? Explain.

2. What is the topic of the essay? Circle the topic in the title.

3. Underline the thesis statement. What organizational pattern does it suggest?

   telling a story   *comparing*   *describing a picture*   *explaining causes*

4. What is the first support paragraph about?

5. What is the second support paragraph about?

6. Why did the writer start a new paragraph in the support section?

7. How many benefits does the writer discuss in the conclusion?

8. Do you agree with the last sentence of the essay? Explain.

B. The paragraphs below are out of order. Write *IP* for introduction paragraph, *SP* for support paragraph, and *CP* for conclusion paragraph.

__SP__ 1.   Some restaurants close because the prices are too high. Some restaurants make good food, but they expect people to pay a lot of money for it. People cannot eat in expensive restaurants often. They usually choose restaurants that are cheap.

_____ 2.   In addition, many restaurants close because the food is not good. Customers have choices. They might try a new restaurant. They will eat one meal, and that meal can have a powerful effect. When food does not taste good, customers feel angry.

_____ 3.   Businesspeople need to understand customers' feelings. To have a successful restaurant, they should give customers good food and a good price. Happy customers have happy memories, and they will return and bring their friends.

_____ 4.   There are successful restaurants in every part of the world. They are next to beaches, on top of buildings, in parks, and even on boats. Many people see popular restaurants and believe that a restaurant is an easy business; however, most restaurants are not successful because their owners make mistakes.

Academic classes have various learning goals, so professors usually give detailed instructions for writing assignments. They often include phrases that help writers organize information.

Phrase	Possible question(s) to answer
give background	Answer *wh-* questions such as *where? when? who?*
compare	What is similar? What is different?
identify causes	Why does (did) something happen?
discuss effects	What changes (changed) after an event?
give reasons *explain why*	Why is something true? How do you know it's true?
summarize	What are the main ideas? (not details)
comment *draw conclusions*	What does the information mean?

In the assignment below, the writer has circled important words and phrases to help her organize her ideas.

Writing Assignment

An effects essay about the positive effects of exercise

Research suggests that exercise has several positive effects on people's health, relationships, and feelings. For this assignment, decide if this is true in your own life.

1. In the **introduction**, give background information about exercise and its effects on people. Then introduce a type of exercise you do, such as taking a walk or running.

2. In the **support paragraph(s)**, give details from your experience to explain each effect in the research. Did your exercise experience match the research? Explain.

3. In the **conclusion**, comment on what you learned from comparing the effects of exercise to your own experience. Do you agree with the research?

A. Read the Writing Assignment below, and circle important words and phrases.

Writing Assignment

An opinion essay about an artist or writer

Artists help people understand the world in a new way. In this assignment, explain why an important artist or writer is special by looking at the person's life and achievements.

1. In the **introduction**, introduce the person and give background information. Write a thesis statement about the person's achievements.

2. In the **support paragraph(s)**, give reasons to support your thesis statement. You can give details from history or the artist's life story. Also include details about the artist's creativity.

3. In your **conclusion**, comment on the artist's influence on art and/or society.

B. Read the model essay below and the words you circled in Activity A. Does the writer complete all parts of the assignment? Explain.

A Magical Writer

Gabriel García Márquez was a famous Colombian writer. He died in 2014, but people still read his books and talk about his talent. He used his life experience and creativity to develop a style of storytelling that was different from other writers' styles.

Márquez grew up in a mountain village in the 1930s. His family had a big house with many relatives. He was close to his grandmother, and she told him many strange stories. In her stories, impossible things happened, but she told them as facts. Later, Márquez combined his grandmother's storytelling style with Colombian history to write books in a style called magic realism.

Magic realism is different from other writing. Márquez's characters are similar to real people with real lives. However, when strange things happen, the characters do not experience them as unusual. For example, a beautiful woman flies into the sky, but no one is surprised.

People like Márquez's style because his writing takes readers into a dream world. While other writers have a similar style, Márquez is the most popular, and his stories have had the biggest effect on readers because they make the impossible seem possible.

C. Work with a partner to ask and answer the questions.

1. After reading about him, do you think Gabriel García Márquez is special? Why?

2. What background details do you learn about him?

3. What is the thesis statement? Underline it.

4. What is the first support paragraph about?

5. How does the writer shift his focus in the second support paragraph?

Writing from Content

Professors also expect students to use information from educational material such as books, classroom lectures, graphs, charts, presentations, maps, and websites to answer questions and support ideas in their writing. In the example below, the content is a graph.

ACADEMIC WRITING TASK Describing climate

Information about temperature and rainfall is important for describing climate. Look at the graph below. What does it say about Seattle's climate?

Work with a partner. Look at the graph. Then check (✓) the questions the graph can answer.

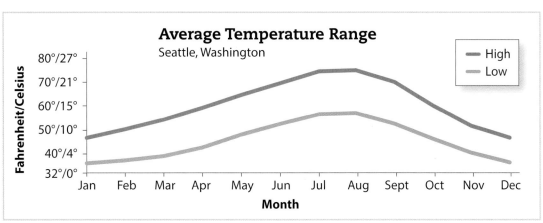

Source: rssWeather.com, accessed November 26, 2014.

_____ 1. What are the hottest months?

_____ 2. What are the coldest months?

_____ 3. How often does it rain?

_____ 4. How is the weather similar or different in winter and in summer?

_____ 5. Does Seattle have a wet climate? Why?

In the Readiness Unit, you reviewed words from *Trio Writing* 1 and 2 and learned new words. Look at the word bank for the Readiness Unit. Check (✓) the words you know. Circle the words you want to learn better.

OXFORD 2000 🔑

Adjectives	Nouns		Verbs	
beautiful	beauty	information	act	improve
comfortable	benefit	motorcycle	affect	include
dangerous	cause	picture	change	provide
difficult	challenge	plan	compare	save
famous	danger	power	depend	see
impossible	development	reason	develop	show
local	effect	society	discuss	start
popular	event	solution	expect	study
possible	exercise	suggestion	explore	suggest
powerful	experience	system	grow	think
successful	influence		help	understand

PRACTICE WITH THE OXFORD 2000 🔑

A. Use the words in the chart. Match adjectives with nouns.

1. _a popular event_   2. _____

3. _____   4. _____

5. _____   6. _____

B. Use the words in the chart. Match verbs with nouns.

1. _provide a solution_   2. _____

3. _____   4. _____

5. _____   6. _____

C. Use the words in the chart. Match verbs with adjective noun partners.

1. _explore possible benefits_   2. _____

3. _____   4. _____

5. _____   6. _____

UNIT **1** Business

CHAPTER 1 — What Company Are You Loyal To?

- Use adjective clauses after objects
- Use adjective clauses after subjects
- Support an opinion essay with reasons
- Use transition words to signal a change of focus
- Write an opinion essay about customer loyalty

▲ VOCABULARY

▶ Oxford 2000 ♪ words to talk about business and customer relationships

A. Write the letter of each group of sentences above the correct picture. Circle the boldfaced words you know. Discuss the words with a partner. Use a dictionary to help you with new words.

a.	b.
Many restaurants **deliver** meals to people's homes.	Small **vehicles** are more **affordable** than large cars and trucks.
Customers **value** the **convenience** of not having to cook.	A motorcycle is **energy efficient** because it does not need a lot of gas.

c.	d.
I am **loyal** to my hairdresser, so I will never change to a different stylist.	When a vehicle **breaks down**, the driver takes it to a repair shop.
Her prices are **affordable**, so I can get a haircut every month.	A good mechanic gets a lot of **repeat business** because people like to take their car to someone they know.

e.	f.
Our neighborhood **gym** has friendly workers and new exercise **equipment**.	Customers value **high-quality** furniture, and they pay extra for it.
The owner knows the **regular** customers' names.	Design **specialists arrange** the pieces of furniture for customers.

1. _____

2. _____

3. _____

4. _____

5. _____

6. _____

B. Ask and answer each question with a partner. Try to use the target vocabulary.

1. A **loyal** customer does not change companies or stores. What does a loyal friend do?

2. Designers **arrange** furniture in stores, and cooks arrange food on plates. What do people who work in a garden arrange?

3. A truck is **convenient** for carrying furniture. What is a car convenient for?

4. Some people **value** comfort and beauty, so they pay extra for the high **quality** of an expensive car. What do people who go to expensive hotels or restaurants value?

5. Will you pay more for a product that is **energy efficient**? Explain.

6. When a clothing store has **repeat business**, it's because customers usually like the **quality** of the clothes. What is usually true about a restaurant with repeat business?

Oxford 2000 🔑

Use the Oxford 2000 list on page 133 to find more words to describe the pictures on these pages. Share your words with a partner.

WORD FORMS

Adjective	Noun	Verb	Adverb
affordable	affordability	afford	
	arrangement	arrange	
convenient	convenience		conveniently
	delivery	deliver	
efficient	efficiency		efficiently
loyal	loyalty		
valuable	value	value	

C. Circle the correct word form to complete each sentence.

1. The restaurant is   *convenient*   (*conveniently*)   located near my house.

2. They have customer   *loyalty*   *loyal*   because they work hard.

3. Designers know how to   *arrangement*   *arrange*   flowers.

4. Quality is   *valuable,*   *value,*   but it is hard to find.

5. An important   *convenient*   *convenience*   is 24-hour customer support.

6. The company offers special   *delivery*   *deliver*   for people who need products fast.

7. The computer is   *affordable*   *affordability*   because it is small.

8. A good salesperson is   *efficient,*   *efficiently,*   so customers do not have to wait.

D. Complete the sentences about each picture with words from the Word Forms box.

1.

a. Busy people like the ___convenience___ of online shopping because someone delivers the product to them.

b. Online shopping is _____, so many people do not mind waiting for delivery.

2.

a. She has a good job, so she can _____ to buy a new car.

b. A small car is more _____ than a big car because it costs less and uses less gas.

3.

a. My friends and I are _____ to our team.

b. _____ to our team is important in our friendship.

4.

a. The cook _____ the food on the plate beautifully.

b. The _____ of food on the plate is beautiful.

5.

a. The flower shop will _____ flowers to people's homes and offices.

b. Many flower shops offer _____ for customers who cannot bring flowers themselves.

6.

a. Factories use machines to build cars because they are _____.

b. The _____ of the machines helps factories produce vehicles quickly.

GO ONLINE
for more
practice

▲▲ GRAMMAR
► Adjective clauses after objects
► Adjective clauses after subjects

A. Read the essay below. What three things did the writer like about his Honda motorcycle?

How a Motorcycle Hooked Me

Honda is a famous Japanese company that makes a variety of vehicles, including cars, trucks, and motorcycles. There are many repeat customers who buy only Hondas. I am also loyal to Honda because I always have a good experience with their vehicles.

My first Honda was a small motorcycle. After I got my first job, I needed a way to get to work. My friend knew someone who had a Honda motorcycle for sale, so I bought it.

The bike was perfect for me in many ways. First, I could move through traffic and park it anywhere. Also, the motorcycle saved me money because it did not use a lot of gas. Third, it was powerful. I could ride up mountains with three people on my motorcycle.

Later, I moved to the United States, and I needed a car that was energy efficient and affordable, so I bought a Honda. It was a good car, so I am a loyal Honda customer.

B. Circle the letter of the clause that best completes each sentence about the essay in Activity A.

1. The writer is someone

   a. who is loyal to Honda.   b. who likes expensive vehicles.

2. The writer likes vehicles

   a. that are fuel efficient.   b. that are big and fast.

3. The writer is someone

   a. who values safety.   b. who values affordability.

4. The writer is proud to own a vehicle

   a. that makes his life easy.   b. that costs a lot of money.

Adjective clauses after objects

Writers often use adjective clauses to add information about nouns. The following sentences have adjective clauses after object nouns.

object noun   adjective clause

I need <u>shoes</u> **that are comfortable for walking.**

I know a <u>designer</u> **who sells affordable furniture.**

An adjective clause has a subject and verb. Use the pronoun *who* to represent a subject that is a person or people. The verb agrees with the noun being described.

who represents **repairman,** so the verb is singular

I have a <u>repairman</u> **who fixes things quickly.**

who represents **people,** so the verb is plural

The company works with <u>people</u> **who build furniture by hand.**

Use the pronoun *that* to represent an object that is a thing or place.

Most customers want affordable <u>clothes</u> **that are also fashionable.**

I usually go to an electronics <u>store</u> **that has very good customer service.**

GO ONLINE
for more
practice

C. Underline the noun for each adjective clause below. Then circle the correct verb to complete the sentence.

1. I found a <u>shop</u> that   *sell*   ⟨*sells*⟩   tea from different countries.

2. I take my car to a nice man who   *own*   *owns*   a repair shop near my house.

3. Customers are loyal to companies that   *give*   *gives*   jobs to local people.

4. In the summer, people usually eat at restaurants that   *have*   *has*   outdoor tables.

5. The best salespeople are the ones who   *do not hurry*   *does not hurry*   customers.

6. I need a phone service that   *have*   *has*   good tech support.

D. Write the letter of the correct clause to complete each sentence.

__f__ 1. I need an intelligent salesperson

_____ 2. In expensive restaurants, there are servers

_____ 3. I joined a gym

_____ 4. My friends introduced me to a travel website

_____ 5. The company has a specialist

_____ 6. There is a shoe company

a. that has affordable exercise classes.

b. that offers good deals at its stores.

c. that compares prices on airplane tickets.

d. who shows people how to use the equipment.

e. who tell customers about the food.

f. ~~who can explain the software to me.~~

Grammar Note

Adjective clauses after subjects

Writers also use adjective clauses after nonspecific subject nouns, such as *people*, *customers*, and *students*, to help define the subject. The verb in the adjective clause agrees with the subject.

subject noun   adjective clause   the verb phrase that completes the sentence

People **who like to watch sports** *need high-quality televisions.*

The adjective clause tells what kind of people need high-quality televisions.

An _airline_ **that runs on time** *has more customer loyalty.*

Writers often use *there is/there are* to introduce a subject and add an adjective clause to give more information about the subject.

subject noun   adjective clause

There are _stores_ **that specialize in computer games.**

The adjective clause tells what kind of stores.

There is _an old man_ **who is very good at repairing watches.**

GO ONLINE
for more practice

E. Circle the correct clause to complete each sentence.

1. People who climb mountains   ~~need special equipment.~~
    needs special equipment.

2. A store that smells good   have more repeat business.
    has more repeat business.

3. There are coffee shops   that stay open all night.
    that stays open all night.

4. There is an app   that help people find affordable hotels.
    that helps people find affordable hotels.

5. A server who knows customers' names   make more money.
    makes more money.

F. Use the words in the charts to write sentences with adjective clauses.

I appreciate companies that have good customer service.

I am loyal to stores		offer tech support
I appreciate companies		have good customer service
There are websites		save customers money
	that	
There is a restaurant		looks beautiful
I know an affordable café		is convenient
I found a small place		has great food

Customers who want good service pay extra.

People		learn about prices	often shop online
Customers	who	get good deals	pay extra
Shoppers		want good service	save money
		are careful	feel proud

Chant

GO ONLINE
for the
Chapter 1
Vocabulary &
Grammar Chant

▲▲▲ **WRITING**
► Supporting an opinion essay with reasons
► Transition words to signal a change of focus

Writing Assignment

An opinion essay about customer loyalty

Customer loyalty is important for a company's success. Think about a company that has repeat business. (Think about companies that *you* like.) Then write an essay explaining what makes customers loyal to that company.

1. In the **introduction**, give background information about the company. What product or service does it sell? Where is it? How big is it?

2. In the **support paragraph(s)**, explain what you like about the company. Give examples of people or services that make the company special.

3. In the **conclusion**, explain why the business has customer loyalty.

Step 1 PREPARE

A. Read Yasmeen's essay. What is the Big Blue Box? Why does it make a good title?

The Big Blue Box

IKEA is a successful furniture company that has stores all over the world. People know the stores because they look like big blue boxes. The word *IKEA* is like *idea*, and the company has many good ideas that have helped customers.

First, IKEA is convenient. People who want to furnish a house or apartment can buy everything they need in one place. Also, customers do not pay someone to assemble what they buy. They buy the furniture in a box and put it together at home. This convenience makes the products perfect for students and people who want to save money.

Second, the furniture has a good design. It is easy to put together, and the pieces match. People enjoy building it. There are also different colors and sizes. Customers who live in small spaces can arrange the furniture in different ways.

In conclusion, people like to save money, but they also want quality. IKEA has customer loyalty because the company gives customers a lot of value for their money.

B. Answer the questions about the essay in Activity A.

1. Why is the name *IKEA* special?

_____

2. What is the first reason why IKEA has customer loyalty? What is the evidence?

_____

_____

3. What is the second reason why IKEA has customer loyalty? What is the evidence?

_____

_____

4. What kind of customer is loyal to IKEA?

_____

5. Do you have the same or different reasons when you shop for products? Why?

_____

Writing Strategy

Supporting an opinion essay with reasons

An opinion is different from a fact because you can disagree with an opinion or have a different understanding, but it is not possible to disagree with a fact.

Consequently, when writers want to share an opinion, they use reasons to support it. An essay organized to introduce and support an opinion has the following parts.

The **introduction** gives background information.
- It answers *who, where, when,* and *what* questions about the topic.
- A thesis statement gives the writer's opinion and focuses the essay.

The **support paragraph(s)** introduce the reasons that support the thesis statement.
- Each reason is introduced and followed by information that includes facts and/or examples.
- Signal words show shifts from one reason to another.
- Reasons with a lot of support are in separate paragraphs.

The **conclusion** brings the opinion and the reasons together.
- The writer may comment on what the opinion means.
- The writer may comment on how the opinion is useful.

GO ONLINE
for more
practice

C. Read Lin's essay below. Underline the thesis statement. What are her two reasons for the statement?

Strong's Gym

1   Strong's Gym is a popular place for people who like to exercise. It has something for everybody, including exercise equipment and classes. However, the gym has customer loyalty for two reasons that people do not always think about.

2   First, the gym is clean and nice. The workout area has new equipment. There are windows, so people can see the garden while they are working out. The gym provides towels and water for guests.

3   Second, the people who work there are polite and helpful. They greet regular guests by name and offer to help. Also, many guests know each other, so there is a feeling of community.

4   In conclusion, repeat business is important for a gym. Strong's Gym has regular customers because the owner pays attention to details. The gym is clean and friendly, so people are happy.

D. Read Lin's comments about her goals below. Write the number of the essay paragraph(s) from Activity C next to each statement.

_3_ 1. I wanted to show that polite workers are important for a successful business.

_____ 2. I wanted the reader to think about why it is important for customers to keep coming back.

_____ 3. I decided to focus on the environment.

_____ 4. I introduced the name of the business, the customers, and the service.

_____ 5. I tried to write a thesis statement that made readers continue reading.

A. Think about businesses that you like. What products or services do they sell? Where are they? How big are they? Write your notes in the chart below. Then choose one for your Writing Assignment.

Stores/products	Technology/apps and electronics	Entertainment/ restaurants/gyms

B. Read the parts of the Writing Assignment on page 28 again. Circle important words and phrases that help you organize your information. Then write notes about your topic for each section.

Introduction First, give background information about the company. What product or service does it sell? Where is it? How big is it?	
Support paragraph(s) In the main part of the essay, explain what you like about the company. Give examples of people or services that make the company special. Do you want to use one or two paragraphs?	
Conclusion Explain why the company has customer loyalty.	

A. Look at your notes from Prewrite. Complete the sentences below about your topic. Then choose the ones you want to use for your background and topic sentences and thesis statement.

Word Partners

pay attention to customers

pay attention to price

pay attention to quality

pay attention to details

pay attention to the environment

GO ONLINE
to practice
word partners

Introduction Background sentences	… is popular because… … is a business that…
Thesis statement	… has customer loyalty because it does several things well. … is popular because it is good at…
Support paragraph(s) Topic sentence(s)	People like… because… First, the company is good at… / First, the customers like… Second, the company offers… / Second, customers appreciate…
Conclusion Concluding sentence	In conclusion, … gets repeat business because… In conclusion, success happens when a company pays attention to…

 B. Write your essay. Use your notes and the Writing Assignment on page 28 to help guide your writing. Add a title.

A. Read the essay. What do people like about Venus Hair?

A Neighborhood Business

Venus Hair is a small neighborhood shop. The place is old, and it has only three chairs. However, the customers are loyal because they feel happy there.

First, the owner, Venus, offers customers a friendly experience. In her small shop, there is always conversation. There are people who know each other, and there are new people who are learning about the neighborhood. They all share information and make jokes.

Venus also does many things for her customers. She is good at cutting hair, so customers look nice. She also keeps prices low, so people can afford her services. For some customers, Venus is more than a hairstylist. In fact, she often drives one customer to her doctor.

Venus Hair has customer loyalty because Venus is the kind of person who pays attention to people. People can gather and have a good time while they get a nice, affordable haircut.

B. Read the essay in Activity A again. Circle *however* and *in fact*.

Writing Strategy

Transition words to signal a change of focus

Writers use transition words to signal new ideas in paragraphs. The following are a few examples:

however: Use this word to signal a contrast.

Doctor Asgari is expensive. ***However,*** *people do not stop seeing her.*

first, second, third: Use these words to signal new supporting ideas.

The restaurant is successful for several reasons. ***First,*** *it is affordable.*

later: Use this word to show a change in time.

I had good experiences in my hometown. ***Later,*** *I moved to the United States.*

in fact: Use *in fact* to show a surprising detail.

People like the food. ***In fact,*** *many customers come several times a week.*

in addition: Use *in addition* to add a new or third reason or point.

The shop is convenient. It is also affordable. ***In addition,*** *the flowers are beautiful.*

GO ONLINE
for more
practice

C. Circle the letter of the sentence with the correct transition word.

1. There are many restaurants that are closer to people's homes.

   a. However, people travel a long way to eat at Tio's.

   b. In addition, people travel a long way to eat at Tio's.

2. There are several good things about Jade. It has a nice environment. Also, the servers are friendly.

   a. In addition, the food is fresh and delicious.

   b. However, the food is spicy and delicious.

3. The theater is special in many ways.

   a. In fact, it has a restaurant downstairs.

   b. First, it has 24 different screens for watching movies.

4. I went to the shop with my mother when I was young.

   a. In addition, I took my children there when I became a mother.

   b. Later, I took my children there when I became a mother.

5. The hotel has a famous history.

   a. Later, people can read customer comments.

   b. In fact, many filmmakers have used it in movies.

6. Students can buy a small car when they do not have a lot of money.

   a. Also, they can sell it and buy a bigger one.

   b. Later, they can sell it and buy a bigger one.

 D. Exchange essays with a partner. Ask and answer the questions below to help each other with ideas. Rewrite your essay.

Oxford 2000 🔑

Do you need more words to write about the business you like? Use the Oxford 2000 list on page 133 to find more words for your essay.

Revising Questions

- What were your goals for the introduction, support paragraphs, and conclusion of your essay?

- How can you use paragraphing skills to develop your ideas?

- What transition words did you use to signal shifts in focus?

- Did you use Oxford 2000 words in your essay?

Step 5 EDIT

A. Read the essay. Find and correct eight mistakes. The first mistake is corrected for you.

Popcap

Popcap is a company ^that^ makes apps and computer games. The games are fun and affordable. Addition, the company have customers all over the world. The company is successful because are designers who make fun games.

All Popcap games have a similar organization. Players first always have a goal. For example, they have to climb or run or take care of something. Second, there is something who is trying to stop them. It can be an animal or a machine, and they have to escape.

In conclusion, there is many companies that make good game apps. In fact, Popcap is special because the designers use beautiful art and interesting stories to do something extra.

 B. Read your essay again. Check (✓) the things in your paragraphs.

Editing Checklist

○ 1. Capital letters, periods, and commas   ○ 2. Adjective clauses after objects

○ 3. Adjective clauses after subjects   ○ 4. Transition words

 C. Now write your final essay. Use the Editing Checklist to help you.

Step 6 PUBLISH

 Follow these steps to publish your paragraphs.

Publishing Steps

- Share your essay with a partner.
- Answer the questions.
  - What details make the business special or different from other businesses?
  - Did the writer give reasons that are important to you as a customer?
- Put your essay in your portfolio!

Critical Thinking Question

Are companies more successful when they also try to help people or the environment?

How Has a Product Changed the World?

- Use the present perfect to connect the past to the present
- Use *or* to show different possibilities or choices
- Compare the past and the present
- Use the present perfect with *as a result*
- Write a comparison essay about a successful product

▲ VOCABULARY ► Oxford 2000 ♪ words to talk about new products on the market

A. Write the letter of each group of sentences above the correct picture. Circle the boldfaced words you know. Discuss the words with a partner. Use a dictionary to help you with new words.

a.	b.
A traveler **invented** the rolling suitcase because he did not want to carry his suitcase.	A new kind of **printer** has **appeared on the market.**
He had an **opportunity** to sell his **invention** to a company.	The technology can make or **copy objects** such as a cup or a toy.

c.	d.
The company **developed** a **process** for turning sunlight into energy.	Some customers use **apps** on their **devices** to find and share the **location** of food trucks.
Its success was a **relief** for many engineers because they did not know if it would work.	Most food trucks specialize in something unusual such as international food or **desserts**.

e.	f.
People quickly **adapted** to GPS devices because they were easy to use.	There are special products for people who have **disabilities**, such as not being able to walk or hear well.
The technology **improved** people's **ability** to find addresses quickly and efficiently.	When older people get hearing **aids**, they are often **relieved** because they can have conversations.

1. _____

2. _____

3. _____

4. _____

5. _____

6. _____

B. Ask and answer each question with a partner. Try to use the target vocabulary.

1. Is it easy or difficult for you to **adapt** to new software? Explain.

2. What are three **objects** that you usually take to school or work?

3. After you travel, are you **relieved** when you get home? Explain.

4. What kind of **dessert** do you like?

5. What is your **process** for packing a **suitcase**?

6. What did you think when electric cars **appeared on the market**?

7. When was the last time you made a **copy** of something? What was it?

8. Why is **location** important when you buy a house?

Oxford 2000 🗝

Use the Oxford 2000 list on page 133 to find more words to describe the pictures on these pages. Share your words with a partner.

WORD FORMS

Some adjectives are formed by adding -ed to the verb. These are called participle adjectives.

Adjective	Noun	Verb
	appearance	appear
designer	design/designer	design
	development	develop
	location	locate
printed	printer	print
relieved	relief	relieve
inventive	invention	invent
improved	improvement	improve

C. Complete each set of sentences with the phrases from the box.

improved the appearance	appeared in stores

1. The company introduced its smartphone in new colors that

   __improved the appearance__ .

2. When smartphones first _____ , customers stood in long lines to buy them.

are relieved	feels relief

3. Customers _____ when someone helps them with their technology.

4. A business owner _____ when she sells a lot of products.

old design	designed educational software

5. The _____ was smaller and less energy efficient.

6. The company _____ that helps children learn about clean energy.

D. Use the words to describe each picture in two separate sentences.

1.

   the improved umbrella / an improvement

   The improved umbrella is better at
   keeping people dry. The new design is an
   improvement because you don't have to carry it.

2.

   the appearance of food trucks / appeared on the street

   _____

   _____

   _____

3.

   designs dresses / a fashion designer

   _____

   _____

   _____

4.

   the location of the / is located on

   _____

   _____

   _____

5.

   a fun invention / invent games that

   _____

   _____

   _____

6.

   felt relieved / it was a big relief when

   _____

   _____

   _____

GO ONLINE
for more
practice

▲▲ GRAMMAR
► Present perfect to connect the past to the present
► *or* to show different possibilities or choices

A. Read the essay below. What kind of relief is the writer describing? Check (✓) the picture that describes the problem in the essay.

Relief

Many older people have problems hearing. Also, people who have worked in noisy environments for a long time can become hard of hearing. In fact, one in five people needs help with hearing.

In the past, people who had hearing problems had to ask a lot of questions during conversations. They could not understand movies, listen to the radio, or share stories. Their disability meant that they often lived lonely lives. For example, some grandparents could not talk to their grandchildren.

The invention of hearing aids has changed the lives of millions of people. Hearing aids have brought relief and happiness to many people who cannot hear well on their own. Now, workers can keep their jobs, and older people can enjoy family life.

B. Read the summary sentences for the paragraphs in the essay in Activity A. Then number them in the same order as the essay.

_____ a. Hearing aids have improved the lives of people with hearing problems.

_____ b. Many people have hearing problems.

_____ c. People with hearing disabilities faced many challenges in the past.

Grammar Note

Present perfect to connect the past to the present

Writers often use the present perfect in a conclusion to explain how something that happened or started in the past affects the present.

something happened in the past that affects the present   **the present**

*When people **have lost** their hearing, they cannot listen to conversations.*

The present perfect uses *has* or *have (not)* + the past participle.

*The company **has improved** the design, and it looks much better.*

*New equipment **has brought** relief to people with disabilities.*

*Rolling suitcases **have made** life easier for travelers. They do not have to carry heavy suitcases.*

Past participles can be regular or irregular.

	Regular past participles	Irregular past participles	
have has	adapted developed changed complained created improved started	become been bought broken brought built done eaten	gone heard left lost made seen written

GO ONLINE
for more
practice

C. Write *agree, partly agree,* or *disagree* next to the present perfect statements about computers below. Then explain your opinions to a partner.

1. _____ Young people have adapted to computer games very well, but older people sometimes have problems.

2. _____ Smartphones have become important in business and education.

3. _____ Many relatives have developed better connections with one another because of technology.

4. _____ Social networking has changed the way people get news.

5. _____ Changes in transportation have improved cities.

6. _____ Technology has changed society in good and bad ways.

D. Use the words in the chart to write sentences.

Parents have expected the company to improve the product.

Young people Customers Shoppers Parents	have (not)	been happy with the game bought the equipment complained about the price expected the company to improve the product
The equipment The product The vehicle The medicine	has (not)	been popular with disabled people made a lot of money for the company brought relief to sick people helped small businesses

Grammar Note

or to show different possibilities or choices

Writers use *or* to show different possibilities or choices.

> *People can drink a cup of coffee **or** tea.*

Use *or* between words and phrases.

> *People can shop online **or** in stores.*

Also, use *or* (not *and*) between words when both reflect a negative condition.

> *They could not listen to the radio **or** watch television.*

Use a comma before *or* when you join two sentences to make a compound sentence.

> *A food truck can go to the same place every day, **or** it can try different places.*

GO ONLINE
for more
practice

E. Circle the letter of the sentence that best completes each compound sentence.

1. Many disabled people had to ask for help, or

   a. they stayed home.

   b. they could not do things by themselves.

2. People had to spend a lot of money on a printer, or

   a. they could keep it in their home for convenience.

   b. they had to go to a special store to make copies.

3. Small business owners paid someone to make a website, or

    a. they did it themselves.

    b. they did not need special programming skills.

4. Before GPS devices, people had to use a map, or

    a. they had to stop and ask for directions.

    b. they looked for the address.

5. Before lifejackets, someone had to hold a child in the water, or

    a. the child was safe.

    b. the child had to learn to swim.

6. In the old days, people stayed home to wait by the phone, or

    a. they did not go out.

    b. they missed calls.

F. Check (✓) each compound sentence, and add a comma if one is needed.

_✓_ 1. Customers can watch a video for help, or they can call customer service.

_____ 2. The glasses come in black or blue with a gold design.

_____ 3. People had to send letters or they had to pay a lot of money to talk on a telephone.

_____ 4. Before Shazaam, people had to learn about music from their friends or wait for someone to say the name of the musician on the radio.

_____ 5. When they wanted to deliver a message, office workers had to walk or make a phone call.

_____ 6. Travelers rode trains or they drove cars.

G. Complete the sentences with your own ideas. Write a complete sentence when there is a comma.

1. It is important to keep food cold, or _it will go bad._

2. When people drink tea, they often add milk or _____

3. On their day off, people usually go to the beach, or _____

4. At lunch, I usually go to a restaurant, or _____

5. Public transportation is good for people who do not have a motorcycle or

_____

Chant

GO ONLINE
for the
Chapter 2
Vocabulary &
Grammar Chant

Writing Assignment

A comparison essay about a successful product

The personal computer is one example of a product that has changed the world. For this assignment, identify a different product that solved a problem. To get ideas, think about your own experiences. What product or service has improved your life?

1. In the **introduction**, give background information about the product or service and how it fits into people's lives.

2. In the **support paragraph(s)**, describe what life was like before the product came on the market. What did people do? What was difficult for them? How did the product solve a problem or fill a need or want?

3. In the **conclusion**, compare the past and the present by commenting on how people have adjusted to the product. Has it become a regular part of life? Why? How?

Step 1 PREPARE

A. Read Kuma's essay. Do you agree that the invention in the essay created a big change? Why or why not?

Wheels for Travel

1 Recently, we found my grandparents' old suitcases upstairs. They were large and square. I imagined my grandfather in the past. In my mind, he was wearing his dark suit and carrying two heavy suitcases. It was a strange image because today, most suitcases look different.

2 Fifty years ago, all travelers carried their suitcases. They often had to stop and change hands or rest. It was hard for people who were not strong. Then someone had the idea for a suitcase with wheels. A company made the first rolling suitcases for airport workers. Later, the company improved the design and lowered the price. At last, the rolling suitcase became affordable for the general public.

3   Now, people have adapted to the freedom of a rolling suitcase. They can travel with heavier bags. A few people use the old style of suitcase, but it has almost disappeared because the new one has made traveling more convenient.

B. Write the number of each paragraph in the essay in Activity A next to the picture that it best matches.

Writing Strategy

Comparing the past and the present

Writers often compare the past and the present to explain a change. An essay organized in this way generally has the following parts.

The **introduction** introduces the topic and tells about the past.
- A thesis statement introduces the change.
- It uses mainly past tenses.

The **support paragraph(s)** describe the change.
- Supporting details give facts, examples, and specific information.
- They use mainly past tenses and sometimes *could* in explanations.

The **conclusion** shifts the focus to the present.
- A conclusion explains why the change is interesting or important today.
- It often uses a combination of the present and the present perfect.

GO ONLINE
for more
practice

C. Read the essay below. Choose the correct introduction sentence from the box for each paragraph. Write it on the line.

> Now, eating at food trucks has become normal.
>
> Street food was different in the past.
>
> The food trucks changed workers' lunch hours in three ways.

Food Trucks

(a) _____ When I worked in Vietnam, I often ate bowls of hot soup or other street food for lunch. However, when I came to the United States, I noticed that workers usually went to restaurants, so I did that too. Then food trucks appeared at many downtown locations and provided a great new service.

(b) _____ First, people did not have to wait. They could stand in line, get their food, and eat it on a bench. They also saved money because the food truck owner did not have many expenses and could charge less. Finally, the food trucks offered interesting food because many cooks were from different countries.

(c) _____ Customers like discovering new food, and they love getting a good deal quickly and easily. Many food trucks have become successful businesses because they make life easy for people during their busy lunchtime.

D. Read the essay in Activity C again. Then write the letter of the writer's goal on the right in the blank on the left.

_____ 1. The introduction

a. I tried to give evidence to explain how food trucks filled a need for workers.

_____ 2. The support

b. I used a comparison of the past and the present to show how food trucks changed how people have lunch.

_____ 3. The conclusion

c. I explained my experience with street food in my country and then connected that to the new idea of food trucks.

_____ 4. All the paragraphs together

d. I shifted to the present tense to show how things are different now than they were in the past.

A. Think about important products or services that have been introduced in your lifetime. Use the photographs below to help you. Write your notes in the chart below. Then choose one for your Writing Assignment.

Software	Products	Services

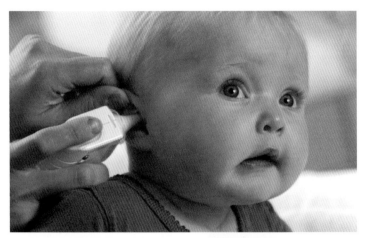

B. Read the parts of the Writing Assignment on page 44 again. Circle important words and phrases that help you organize your information. Then write notes about your topic for each section.

Introduction Start with a short description of the product or service. How does it fit into people's lives or the modern world?	
Support paragraph(s) Describe what life was like before the product came on the market. What did people do? What was difficult for them? How did the product solve a problem or fill a need or want? Do you want to use one or two paragraphs?	
Conclusion Compare the past and the present by commenting on how people have adapted to the product. Has it become a regular part of life? Why? How?	

Step 3 WRITE

Word Partners

brought relief

brought new ideas

brought (something) to the market

brought about a change

brought success (to)

GO ONLINE
to practice
word partners

A. Look at your notes from Prewrite. Complete the sentences below about your topic. Then choose the ones you want to use for your background and topic sentences and thesis statement.

Introduction Background sentences	In the past, people used to... Before... people used to...
Thesis statement	Then... appeared. People needed a new...
Support paragraph(s) Topic sentence(s)	The change happened quickly/slowly. ... changed the market/product in... ways.
Conclusion Concluding sentence	Now, ... is normal. These days, ... is everywhere.

 B. Write your essay. Use your notes and the Writing Assignment on page 44 to help guide your writing. Add a title.

A. Read the essay. Does everyone need a 3D printer?

3D for Everyone

Many people like to invent things, but it is hard to turn an idea into an object. Usually it takes special equipment, time, and skills to build examples. However, the appearance of 3D printers has changed the way inventors work.

Before 3D printers, companies had to pay workers to build models when they wanted to develop a new product. The first 3D printers helped companies build parts and test ideas. When the price for the printers went down, smaller businesses could afford them. Then regular people started using the printers to design jewelry or the parts of an object that they wanted to build, such as a toy.

At first, many people thought the idea was crazy, but the public adapted to the new technology; as a result, 3D printers have become a regular part of life. They have changed the world because now anybody can invent things, solve problems, or start a new business.

B. Read the essay in Activity A again. Circle *as a result*.

Writing Strategy

Present perfect with *as a result*
Writers often use the transition phrase *as a result* with a present perfect sentence to show an effect that started in the past and continues.

Generally, use a period when *as a result* explains several sentences.

Companies started making sports equipment for people with disabilities. Then leagues for players with disabilities were formed. As a result, many people with special needs have become more active.

Generally, use a semicolon when *as a result* explains one sentence.

The city built bicycle lanes downtown; as a result, people have started to ride their bikes to work.

GO ONLINE
for more
practice

C. Work with a partner. Use the present perfect to complete the sentences with effects.

1. The company worked hard on the design. Also, it offered the new computers at a fair

   price. As a result, _many people have bought them._____

2. Gas is expensive this year; as a result, _____

3. Many people want to save money; as a result, _____

4. Many children play computer games; as a result, _____

5. There are many free or affordable apps; as a result, _____

 D. Exchange essays with a partner. Ask and answer the questions below to help each other with ideas. Rewrite your essay.

Oxford 2000 🔑

Do you need more words to write about a successful product? Use the Oxford 2000 list on page 133 to find more words for your essay.

Revising Questions

- What were your goals for the different parts of your essay?
- How can you use paragraphing skills to develop your ideas?
- How did you compare the past to the present?
- Did you use Oxford 2000 words in your essay?

Step 5 EDIT

A. Read the essay. Find and correct seven mistakes. The first mistake is corrected for you.

Flying Cameras

television or

When people watch sports on ~~television, or~~ on their computers, they do not always think about the photography equipment. They only enjoy the game. However, sports photography has improvement because flying cameras can show the best parts of a game.

50   Unit 1 | Chapter 2

Before flying cameras, photographers tried to show the important action of a game, but they could not go on the field. They had to use special cameras. Or they had to be lucky. Most of the pictures were far away or they were not clear. When technology companies introduced small flying robots, news organizations connected cameras to the robots and used them to get better pictures of games.

Now, robots have start to do most of the photography. They do not bother the athletes, and they can follow the action; as result, people who watch sports at home expect to see the important moments of the game up close. People has adapted easily because the cameras met a need.

 B. Read your essay again. Check (✓) the things in your paragraphs.

Editing Checklist

○ 1. Capital letters, periods, and commas ○ 2. Present perfect to connect the past to the present

○ 3. *or* to show different possibilities or choices ○ 4. Present perfect with *as a result*

 C. Now write your final essay. Use the Editing Checklist to help you.

Step 6 PUBLISH

 Follow these steps to publish your paragraphs.

Publishing Steps

- Share your essay with a partner.
- Answer the questions.
  - What do you know about this product or service?
  - Did the writer make it clear that the product or service solves a problem or fills a need or want?
- Put your essay in your portfolio!

Critical Thinking Question

What are the effects of *not* having a smartphone?

CHAPTER 3 Interpreting a Flow Chart

- Interpret a flow chart about consumer behavior
- Use business and marketing words and phrases
- Make connections
- Practice using academic content in a short writing task

ACADEMIC CONTENT: A flow chart about consumer behavior

A. Think of the last time you spent money on something important. Then ask and answer each question.

1. How did you research information about the product before you bought it?

2. What did you think about before you bought the product?

3. Were you happy with your choice? Why or why not?

B. The flow chart below shows the process people go through when they buy something. Write the letter of the summary sentence next to the correct stage in the five-stage model.

The Five-Stage Model

_____ Problem recognition

_____ Information search

_____ Evaluation of alternatives

_____ Purchase decision

_____ Postpurchase behavior

Source: "5 Steps to Understanding Your Customer's Buying Process," Euan Johnston, June 24, 2013, www.b2bmarketing.net

Interpretation

a. The consumer thinks about different choices.

b. The consumer realizes that he/she needs to buy something.

c. The consumer thinks about what he/she has bought.

d. The consumer gets information about the product and sellers.

e. The consumer decides to buy the product.

C. Check the sentences that describe the process you used when buying the product you talked about in Activity A. Use "Other" to add your own sentences if needed.

1. Problem recognition

_____ I wanted it for fun.

_____ I needed it to achieve a goal.

_____ I needed to buy a gift for someone.

Other: _____

2. Information search

_____ I talked to people.

_____ I looked online.

_____ I went to stores.

Other: _____

3. Evaluation of alternatives

_____ I thought about price.

_____ I thought about quality.

_____ I thought about why I needed it.

Other: _____

4. Purchase decision

_____ I bought it suddenly without a plan.

_____ I made a plan and went to a store.

_____ I ordered it to be delivered.

Other: _____

5. Postpurchase behavior

_____ I returned the item.

_____ I was not happy, but I did not return it.

_____ I was happy with my purchase.

Other: _____

Language Focus

Business and marketing words and phrases

Language	Definition	Example sentence
come on the market	a new product is for sale	A new type of energy-efficient car has **come on the market.**
consumer behavior	customers' actions before, during, and after buying a product	Companies study **consumer behavior** so they can get more customers and sell more products.
purchase (v.) make a purchase (n.)	buy something	People **purchase** products and services for different reasons.
postpurchase	an action after buying something	A consumer's **postpurchase** behavior affects a company.
problem recognition	to realize that one needs something to solve a problem	**Problem recognition** gets buyers to think about something they need.
marketing	making people want to buy a product or service	Putting advertisements in magazines is a **marketing** strategy.
increase sales	sell more of something	Companies try to **increase sales** by lowering prices.

GO ONLINE
for more
practice

D. Write the word or phrase from the Language Focus that fits each meaning.

1. ___problem recognition___ A student realizes that she needs a computer for school.

2. _____ A customer returned the shoes to the store because she did not like them.

3. _____ Many people buy a new phone, and the company makes a lot of money.

4. _____ A company advertises to find customers for a product.

5. _____ A woman buys jewelry at a store or online.

6. _____ A company introduces a new flavor of ice cream.

7. _____ Friends go shopping, give each other advice, and then buy some clothes.

PREWRITE

A. Read the Academic Writing Task below. Circle the words and phrases that give directions. Then use the Prewrite activities to plan your assignment.

ACADEMIC WRITING TASK An analysis of purchasing behavior

People usually go through five different stages when they spend money on something important. Apply the five-stage model to a purchase you have made. To complete the assignment, summarize each stage in a short paragraph, and explain your experience at that stage.

B. Think about big purchases you have made, and write notes in the chart. Then choose one for your assignment.

Technology	
Clothing	
Entertainment	

Travel	
Equipment	

Critical Thinking
MAKING
CONNECTIONS

People learn when they make connections. They apply information they learn in one context to a different context.

C. Use your notes from Activity B and the five-stage model to plan the parts of your assignment.

Stage 1: _____

Stage 2: _____

Stage 3: _____

Stage 4: _____

Stage 5: _____

WRITE AND EDIT

A. Use your sentences and ideas from Prewrite to write your assignment. Use the Academic Writing Task on page 54 to help guide your writing.

B. Use the checklist below to review your writing.

Academic Writing Task Checklist

Check (✓) for examples.

○ 1. I summarized the stages of consumer behavior.

○ 2. I explained my experience at each stage.

○ 3. I used marketing language.

○ 4. I used correct grammar, punctuation, and capitalization.

Chant

GO ONLINE
for the
Chapter 3
Vocabulary &
Grammar Chant

Look at the word bank for Unit 1. Check (✓) the words you know. Circle the words you want to learn better.

OXFORD 2000

Adjectives	Nouns		Verbs
broken	ability	equipment	afford
convenient	appearance	market	appear
high	arrangement	object	arrange
regular	business	opportunity	break
special	copy	process	copy
valuable	customer	quality	deliver
	design	relief	design
	development	repair	develop
	device	value	improve
	energy	vehicle	invent
			print
			repair
			repeat

PRACTICE WITH THE OXFORD 2000 🔑

A. Use the words in the chart. Match adjectives with nouns.

1. _a regular customer_   2. _____

3. _____   4. _____

5. _____   6. _____

B. Use the words in the chart. Match verbs with nouns.

1. _develop a business_   2. _____

3. _____   4. _____

5. _____   6. _____

C. Use the words in the chart. Match verbs with adjective noun partners.

1. _design special equipment_   2. _____

3. _____   4. _____

5. _____   6. _____

GO ONLINE
for more
practice

UNIT 2 Science

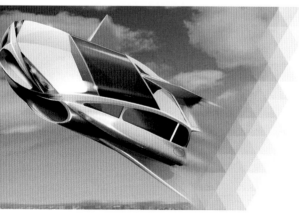

When Did Nature Amaze You?

- Use the past perfect with *so* and *because*
- Use quoted speech
- Introduce a narrative essay

- Use time markers
- Write a narrative essay about an experience in nature

▲ VOCABULARY ▶ Oxford 2000 ⚷ words to talk about experiences in nature

A. Write the letter of each group of sentences above the correct picture. Circle the boldfaced words you know. Discuss the words with a partner. Use a dictionary to help you with new words.

a.	**b.**
The lake was **calm** because there was no wind. A group of birds was **flying through the air**.	**Waves** on the river **were crashing into** our boat. We came to a powerful **waterfall**.
c.	**d.**
We had **an amazing view** because we saw hundreds of **stars**. The stars were **shining brightly** in the night sky.	A **thunderstorm** with dark, gray clouds **appeared in the distance**. **Flashes of lightning** hit the ground.
e.	**f.**
My friends and I **reached the top** of the mountain. It was cold because the sun **had disappeared behind** the clouds.	We stood under a bridge to **escape the heavy rain**. We waited there for the **rough** weather to pass.

1. _____

2. _____

3. _____

4. _____

5. _____

6. _____

B. Ask and answer each question with a partner. Try to use the target vocabulary.

1. What places in nature make you feel **calm** and peaceful?

2. What can make the **stars disappear** at night?

3. When did you see an **amazing** sunset?

4. How do you know when a **thunderstorm** is close to you?

5. When was the last time you experienced **heavy rain**?

Oxford 2000 🔑

Use the Oxford 2000 list on page 133 to find more words to describe the pictures on these pages. Share your words with a partner.

WORD FORMS

Many adverbs are formed by adding *-ly* to the adjective form.

Adjective	Noun	Verb	Adverb
amazing amazed	*amazement*	*amaze*	*amazingly*
	appearance	*appear*	
bright	*brightness*	*brighten*	*brightly*
calm		*calm (down)*	*calmly*
distant	*distance*		
heavy			*heavily*
	view	*view*	

C. Complete each set of sentences with the phrases from the box.

stood in amazement	amazingly beautiful

1. The pink sky was _____amazingly beautiful_____ after the storm.

2. We _____ while we watched the bear catch a fish in the river.

calms me down	walked calmly

3. Being outside in nature always _____.

4. I _____ so that I did not scare the cat away.

bright light	brightly colored

5. The _____ of the morning sun shined through my bedroom window.

6. Hundreds of _____ fish were swimming below us.

disappeared from view	disappearance of

7. The bird flew into the trees and _____.

8. Scientists are worried about the _____ butterflies in some parts of the world.

D. Use the words to describe each picture in two separate sentences.

1.

   a beautiful view of / viewed the sunset

   There was a beautiful view of the sunset.

   She viewed the sunset from her window.

   _____

2.

   heavy coats / snowing heavily

   _____

   _____

   _____

3.

   in the distance / distant mountains

   _____

   _____

   _____

4.

   had a strange appearance / appeared to look

   _____

   _____

   _____

5.

   an amazing place / were amazed by

   _____

   _____

   _____

6.

   bright moon / shining brightly

   _____

   _____

   _____

GO ONLINE
for more
practice

A. Read Sara's essay. How old do you think Sara was? Why?

Starry Night

One winter, my family was traveling to a small town in the mountains. The sun had already set, so the roads were dark. I was sleeping in the car when a cold wind woke me up. My father was standing outside the car in the dark. "Come out, Sara," he said. "I want to show you something."

My father helped me out of the car. Then he pointed at the sky. Hundreds of stars were shining brightly. They were beautiful colors and different sizes. Some of them were close together in bright groups, and others were far apart. Suddenly, I saw one star fly across the sky. I tried to follow it with my eyes, but it had already disappeared into the darkness.

I was amazed because I had never seen the night sky so clearly. The stars were bright because we were far from the city and the air was clear. Later, I thought about the great distance to the stars and the power of nature. It was a beautiful experience, and I will never forget it.

B. Read the sentences about the essay in Activity A. Number the events in the correct order.

_____ a. Sara's father pointed to the stars in the sky.

_____ b. Sara thought about the distance to the stars.

_____ c. Sara's family started driving to the mountains.

_____ d. A star disappeared into the darkness.

_____ e. Sara fell asleep in the car.

Past perfect with *so* and *because*

The past perfect tense shows that one action was completed before a second action.
Writers often use the past perfect tense with *so* and *because* to explain a reason.

reason

*The sun had already set, **so** the roads were dark.*

reason

*We went inside **because** it had begun to rain.*

The past perfect uses *had (not)* + the past participle.

We were tired because we had hiked a long way.
The sun had not set, so we had time to get back home.

GO ONLINE
for more
practice

C. Complete the sentences with the past perfect tense verbs in the box.

had become	had forgotten
had blown	had had
had changed	had heard
had disappeared	had hit

1. The sky ___had become___ dark, so we decided to go inside.

2. We _____ to bring food, so we were hungry.

3. The trees were black because lightning _____ them.

4. We were worried because we _____ thunder.

5. The sun _____ behind the clouds, so the air felt cooler.

6. Our view of the forest _____ because we were higher in the mountains.

7. I was happy because we _____ an amazing time.

8. We were surprised because the wind _____ open our kitchen window.

D. Complete each sentence with the verb in parentheses. Use *had (not)* + the past participle form of the verb.

1. (got) It was easier to see because the sky ___had gotten___ brighter.

2. (appear) We were worried because dark clouds _____ in the distance.

3. (be) I _____ to the top of the mountain before, so I did not know what to expect.

4. (come) Winter _____ , so the days were cold and gray.

5. (change) The trees were orange and red because the leaves _____ color.

6. (bring) We were lost because we _____ a map with us.

Grammar Note

Quoted speech

Writers use quoted speech to write the exact words people said. Use quotation marks (" ") to begin and end a quote. Capitalize the first letter of the quote, and put punctuation inside the quotation mark.

"Please be careful."   *"Look at that!"*
                    "Was that thunder?"

Writers often follow a quote with a subject and a reporting verb such as *said*, *asked*, or *shouted*. The punctuation before the end of the quote is different for each reporting verb.

comma (,)	*"Please be careful,"* my parents **said**. *"I think it's going to be a beautiful day,"* I **said**.
question mark (?)	*"Was that thunder?"* my brother **asked**. *"Are you tired?"* I **asked**.
exclamation point (!)	*"Look at that!"* he **shouted**. *"There's something in those bushes!"* my friend **shouted**.

When writers separate a quote with a reporting verb, the second quote begins a new sentence.

new sentence

"Come out, Sara," he said. *"I want to show you something."*

GO ONLINE
for more
practice

E. Read the sentences. Add quotation marks and correct punctuation.

1. "Let's go home," my friend said.

2. I'm not worried I said.

3. What time is it I asked.

4. Watch out my brother shouted.

5. Do you want to keep going I asked.

6. It's getting dark I said. Let's stop here.

F. Write sentences with the words in parentheses. Use quoted speech and correct punctuation.

1. A flash of lightning lit the sky.

"That was close!" my friend shouted. "Let's go!"
_____

(*that was close / my friend shouted / let's go*)

2. I was pointing to the star, but my son couldn't find it.

_____

(*Look closer / I said*)

3. I smiled nervously and stepped into the boat.

_____

(*are you ready / my father asked*)

4. We were walking through the forest when I heard a strange noise.

_____

(*did you hear that / I asked*)

5. I was worried because the rain was not stopping.

_____

(*I think we'll be fine / my friend said*)

6. My friend was getting too close to the dog.

_____

(*stop / I shouted / he doesn't look friendly*)

Chant

GO ONLINE
for the
Chapter 4
Vocabulary &
Grammar Chant

Writing Assignment

A narrative essay about an experience in nature

Nature can be powerful and unexpected. In this assignment, you will write a narrative essay about an experience in nature that had a powerful effect on you.

1. In the **introduction**, give the setting. When did it happen? Where were you? Who were you with? Include other details about the setting that are important.

2. In the **support paragraph(s)**, describe the experience. In this part, focus on nature, not your feelings. Try to describe it fully by including as many details as you can. What did you see? What did you hear? What happened?

3. In the **conclusion**, explain how the experience made you feel. What did you learn from the experience about yourself or the natural world?

Step 1 PREPARE

A. Read Khiem's narrative essay. How did his experience change his view of the Pacuare River?

On the Pacuare River

One summer, my friends and I decided to take a trip to the Pacuare River in Costa Rica. We got to the river early in the morning. I was excited because I had never tried river rafting, and I didn't know what to expect.

We got in the boat and started rafting. Eventually, we heard rough water ahead of us. "Get ready!" my friend shouted. All of a sudden, the water moved quickly, and powerful waves crashed into our boat. "Look at that!" my friend Sam said. He was pointing to a high waterfall in the distance. At first, it was quiet, but when we reached it, we heard its powerful crash.

It is hard to describe the Pacuare River. In photos, it looks green and calm, but rafting made me view it differently. Now I appreciate its true power, and my friends and I can't wait to go back and experience its dangerous beauty again.

B. Read the summary sentences for the paragraphs in the essay in Activity A. Then number them in the same order as the essay.

_____ a. Rafting made Khiem appreciate the river's power.

_____ b. Khiem and his friends made plans to go river rafting in Costa Rica.

_____ c. Strong water carried their boat down the river to a waterfall.

Writing Strategy

Introducing a narrative essay

A narrative essay describes an experience using details and observations. The introduction often tells the background setting or the time and place of the event. Time phrases such as *one winter, one year,* and *one day* can introduce the setting.

The thesis statement prepares readers for the action of the story. It makes readers curious about a problem or an unexpected situation but doesn't tell about the main event.

Examples:

I was excited because I had never tried river rafting, and I did not know what to expect.

"Come out, Sara," my father said. "I want to show you something."

GO ONLINE
for more
practice

C. Use a phrase from the box to introduce the setting of each introduction. Underline the detail(s) that help describe the setting.

| One evening | One morning | One summer | One winter |

1. _One summer_, my family and I took a vacation to the California coast. The <u>days were hot</u>, but the air was clean, and the ocean smelled beautiful.

2. _____, I was riding my motorcycle to work. It had rained hard the night before, so the streets were wet. There were still some clouds in the sky.

3. _____, my friends and I decided to go skiing in the mountains. The weather was cold, and there was fresh snow on the ground. We stood at the top of the mountain and looked down.

4. _____, I was sitting on my front porch. I had already eaten dinner, and I was enjoying the view of the sunset and the pink clouds in the sky.

D. Read the thesis statements below. Match each thesis statement to the correct setting using the numbers from Activity C.

_____ a. However, I wasn't expecting the clouds to change the way they did.

_____ b. Everything was fine, but then it started to rain again.

_____ c. We stopped at a beach, and I was ready to get in the water.

_____ d. "Ready to go down?" my friend asked.

Step 2 PREWRITE

A. Look at the topics below, and list a personal experience you had with each one. Then choose one for your Writing Assignment.

Topic	Personal Experience
1. a time you saw something unexpected in nature	
2. a time you experienced powerful weather	

B. Read the parts of the Writing Assignment on page 66 again. Circle important words and phrases that help you organize your information. Then write notes about your topic for each section.

Introduction First, give the background setting. When did it happen? Where were you? Who were you with?	
Support paragraph(s) Next, describe the experience. What did you see? What did you hear? What happened? Do you want to use one or two paragraphs?	

Conclusion Finally, explain how the experience made you feel. What did you learn from the experience about yourself or the natural world?	

Step 3 WRITE

A. Look at your notes from Prewrite. Write a sentence that introduces the setting. Use a time phrase such as *one year, one day, one summer*, or your own phrase.

_____

_____

B. Write a thesis statement that prepares readers for the action in your story.

_____

_____

C. Write down what you or other people said during the experience below. Use quoted speech.

Example: "_____Get ready!_____" _____my friend shouted_____.

1. "_____" _____.

2. "_____" _____.

D. Write your essay. Use your notes and the Writing Assignment on page 66 to help guide your writing. Add a title.

Word Partners

an amazing place

an amazing view

an amazing experience

an amazing time

an amazing event

_____

GO ONLINE
to practice
word partners

A. Read the essay. What unexpected event happened?

Desert Adventure

One summer, my friend and I visited a high, flat mountain in the desert. The weather was good, and we enjoyed beautiful views of the red and orange landscape around us. Our day was perfect until it was time to go back.

On our way, I saw a large, dark cloud to my left. It looked strange because the sky over us was still blue. I could see flashes of lightning coming from the cloud. A few minutes later, I heard thunder. "It's good that storm is not here!" my friend said.

Suddenly, the sky over us became gray and purple. We realized that the lightning was getting closer. The storm was moving over us, and there was no escape. We had to sit and wait. It took a long time, but the storm eventually passed.

I was scared because I had never been so close to lightning before. Luckily, we did not get hurt. That day, I realized that the high desert can be a beautiful but dangerous place.

B. Read the essay in Activity A again. Circle *eventually*, *suddenly*, and *still*.

Time markers

In a narrative essay, writers use the adverbs *suddenly*, *eventually*, and *still* to show how they experienced time during an event.

Use *suddenly* to express that you experienced a quick action or change.

*I saw dark clouds above me. **Suddenly**, heavy rain began to fall.*

*A strong wind **suddenly** blew across the desert.*

Use *eventually* to express that you waited for an event or problem to happen.

*We got in the boat and started rafting. **Eventually**, we heard powerful water ahead of us.*

*The sun **eventually** appeared from behind the clouds.*

Use *still* to express that an action or state continued longer than you expected.

*We controlled our boat, but the river was **still** moving fast.*

*We were **still** on the road, and it was getting dark.*

GO ONLINE for more practice

C. Complete each paragraph with *eventually*, *suddenly*, or *still*.

1. The ocean water was calm, and the waves were small. (a) ___Suddenly___, a tall wave appeared in the distance. "That's going to be a big one!" my friend shouted. It looked like a good wave, but it was (b) _____ far away. We waited a couple minutes and watched. (c) _____, it got close to us, and we were ready to jump in.

2. My friend and I got our skis. The sky was gray, and it was (a) _____ snowing. "You ready?" my friend asked. We headed down the mountain, but the snowfall was thick. Then my friend (b) _____ stopped. "I can't see anything!" he said. "Can you?" I looked around, and everything was white. We kept moving and (c) _____ got to the bottom, but it wasn't easy.

D. Exchange essays with a partner. Ask and answer the questions below to help each other with ideas. Rewrite your essay.

Revising Questions

- What were your goals for the different parts of your essay?
- How can you use paragraphing skills to develop your ideas?
- What time markers did you use to show how you experienced time?
- Did you use Oxford 2000 words in your essay?

Oxford 2000 🔑

Do you need more words to write about your experience? Use the Oxford 2000 list on page 133 to find more words for your essay.

A. Read the essay. Find and correct nine mistakes. The first mistake is corrected for you.

Orange and Black

One winter, *comma* my family and I took a trip to a forest in northern Mexico. It still a little dark because we had get up early. "Where are they" my daughter asked.

Eventually we heard them. We looked up, and hundreds of Monarch butterflies were flying through the air. "Look at the trees" my daughter shouted, "They're orange and black!" We stood in amazement because we never seen so many butterflies before. The trees were covered in their beautiful colors, and the forest looked like a painting.

Seeing the Monarch butterflies was an amaze experience. I saw the power of nature, and my daughter saw all of its beauty. It was a special moment that my family and I will never forget.

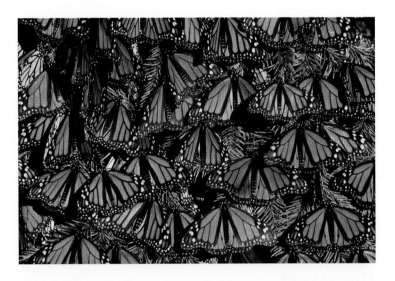

B. Read your essay again. Check (✓) the things in your essay.

Editing Checklist

○ 1. Capital letters, periods, and commas   ○ 2. Past perfect with *so* and *because*

○ 3. Quoted speech   ○ 4. Time markers (e.g., *suddenly, eventually, still*)

C. Now write your final essay. Use the Editing Checklist to help you.

Step 6 PUBLISH

Follow these steps to publish your essay.

Publishing Steps

- Share your paragraphs with a partner.
- Answer the questions.
  - What details make the narrative interesting to read?
  - Have you had a similar experience in nature? When?
- Put your essay in your portfolio!

Critical Thinking Question

What can nature give people? Name three things.

CHAPTER 5

Is Your Energy Use Increasing?

- Use the present progressive to describe current trends
- Use *could, should,* and *will have to*
- Write an essay about causes

- Use *especially* with prepositional phrases
- Write an essay about the causes of energy use

▲ **VOCABULARY** ▸ Oxford 2000 ✦ words to talk about energy use

A. Write the letter of each group of sentences above the correct picture. Circle the boldfaced words you know. Discuss the words with a partner. Use a dictionary to help you with new words.

a.	**b.**
Scientists look for new **sources of oil** below Earth's **surface**. Searching for oil **requires** special devices.	**Solar power** is **energy** from the sun. It **produces electricity** for homes and businesses.
c.	**d.**
Modern **machines collect** energy from the wind. They are good for the environment because they do not **cause pollution**.	The chart **provides** information about **population trends**. The information shows that the number of people living in cities is **increasing**.
e.	**f.**
The northern **region** of the country has a modern city. In contrast, the southern region has old, **traditional** villages.	**Decreasing** the number of cars on the road is a **priority** for the city. The local **citizens** want to help their community. They bike to work so that there is less traffic on the roads.

1. _____

Percent (%) of Population in Cities

2. _____

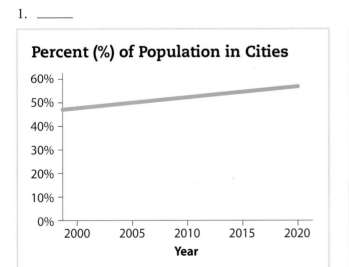

3. _____

4. _____

5. _____

6. _____

B. Ask and answer each question with a partner. Try to use the target vocabulary.

1. What is an important **priority** for the citizens of your country?

2. Is your city's **population increasing** or **decreasing**? Why?

3. How can people save **electricity** at home?

4. Which countries in the world **produce** a lot of **oil**?

5. Which **region** of your country is the most beautiful? Why?

Oxford 2000 🔑

Use the Oxford 2000 list on page 133 to find more words to describe the pictures on these pages. Share your words with a partner.

WORD FORMS

Some nouns are formed by adding *-tion* to the verb form.

Adjective	Noun	Verb	Adverb
	collection	*collect*	
decreasing	*decrease*	*decrease*	*decreasingly*
increasing	*increase*	*increase*	*increasingly*
polluted	*pollution*	*pollute*	
required	*requirement*	*require*	
traditional	*tradition*		*traditionally*

C. Complete each set of sentences with the phrases from the box.

collecting information	a large collection of

1. The city is ____collecting information____ about recent population changes.

2. Our school library has _____ books and videos.

strong traditions	traditionally use

3. People in my country have _____ and beliefs.

4. Villagers _____ wood to heat their homes in the winter.

decrease in	decrease the number

5. The government wants to _____ of cars on the road.

6. There was a _____ the region's population last year.

an increasing number	increasingly important

7. _____ of people are moving to Beijing to find jobs.

8. The world's energy needs have become _____ in the 21st century.

D. Use the words to describe each picture in two separate sentences.

1.
   collect trash / trash collection

   Trucks collect trash.

   Trash collection is important to keep

   cities clean.

2. *a traditional village / a village tradition*

   _____

   _____

   _____

3. *traffic increases / an increase in energy use*

   _____

   _____

   _____

4. *a source of pollution / pollute the air*

   _____

   _____

   _____

5. *require fresh air / another basic requirement*

   _____

   _____

   _____

6. *a decreasing amount of ice /*
   when the amount of ice decreases

   _____

   _____

   _____

GO ONLINE
for more
practice

▲▲ GRAMMAR
▸ Present progressive to describe current trends
▸ *could, should,* and *will have to*

A. Read Kyle's essay. How is the Philippines changing?

Energy in the Philippines

The Philippines is a beautiful country. It is also an old country, and it has many traditional ways. However, the country has begun to change, and today its energy needs are increasing.

One cause of the increase is the population. Neighborhoods are growing fast. As a result, the country has to produce a lot of electricity for homes. Most people use electricity for lighting, watching television, and cooking.

Another cause is transportation. The cities are growing, and people need to travel. There are more cars and motorcycles on the streets. There are also many buses on the road, especially during the day. The buses are old, so they use a lot of gas.

The country's energy needs will keep growing, but Filipinos could do two things. The government buys energy from other countries, but it could make energy from wind. Also, the country could start using modern buses and electric trains. These opportunities could help the Philippines and decrease pollution, too.

B. Read the sentences about the essay in Activity A. Check (✓) the sentences that are true.

_____ 1. The Philippines requires more energy today.

_____ 2. The population in the Philippines is growing.

_____ 3. Buses in the cities use modern technology.

_____ 4. The Philippines gets windy weather.

_____ 5. Kyle believes that electric trains are the only solution.

Grammar Note

Present progressive to describe current trends

Writers often use the present progressive to show how a situation is changing today.

*Today, more people **are using** public transportation.*

*Citizens **are** also **buying** new energy-efficient devices for their homes these days.*

Verbs that explain trends or changes are often used in the present progressive. Some of these verbs include *become, change, decrease, get, grow,* and *increase.*

*My country's energy needs **are changing**.*

*City neighborhoods **are becoming** more modern.*

*These days, the number of people in my hometown **is decreasing**.*

*The population **is getting** smaller.*

The present progressive uses *am/is/are* with the *-ing* form of a verb. Below are two spelling rules to remember when you add *-ing* to certain verbs.

Rule 1: Drop a silent "e."	become ⟶ becoming continue ⟶ continuing use ⟶ using
Rule 2: Double the final consonant with some one-syllable verbs.	dig ⟶ digging get ⟶ getting put ⟶ putting

GO ONLINE for more practice

C. Use the words in the chart to write sentences. Use correct punctuation.

Today, my city is looking for energy solutions.

Today These days	my city countries the population clean energy transportation electronic devices	is are	becoming more popular causing pollution changing getting more expensive growing quickly looking for energy solutions using new sources of energy

D. Complete the sentences with phrases from the box. Use the present progressive tense and the correct spelling of the -*ing* form.

become less healthy	provide homes for birds	save money on electricity
get more crowded	put recycling cans on the sidewalks	use electric buses
make electricity from the sun		

1. The company is using energy-efficient computers, so it

   is saving money on electricity_____.

2. Cars are causing pollution, so air in our region

   _____.

3. Public transportation has changed in Bogota because now the city

   _____.

4. The island of Fiji cannot produce traditional energy, so it

   _____.

5. The city's population is growing. As a result, the streets

   _____.

6. Our community wants to collect plastic, so we

   _____.

7. The new trees that the city planted

   _____.

Grammar Note

could, should, and will have to

Writers use *could*, *should*, and *will have to* when they give advice or a solution for the future. *Could*, *should*, and *will have to* have similar meanings, but they show different feelings.

Use *could* to give possible solutions.	*One solution **could be** to make energy from the wind. Energy **could come** from the sun as well.*

Use *should* when you feel an idea is the best solution.	*The government **should provide** more public transportation so that people have choices.*
Use *will have to* to suggest that there will be no other choice in the future.	*The population is growing, so I believe the city **will have to build** more housing in the future.*

GO ONLINE for more practice

E. Read the topic sentence. Circle the correct support sentence.

1. Traffic into London is heavy, but there is a possible solution.

   a. Coworkers who live close together could drive to work together.

   b. Drivers who live outside of the city will have to use highways.

2. Small villages along the Vietnamese coast could use solar power.

   a. Solar technology is too expensive.

   b. Coastal regions get a lot of sun all year.

3. My family wants to save money on electricity next year.

   a. We should use energy-efficient light bulbs.

   b. We will have to use electronic devices.

4. To decrease pollution, modern cities will have to produce more clean energy.

   a. They could make electricity from the wind.

   b. They could make electricity from oil and gas.

5. I think that governments should help businesses that use less energy.

   a. They could decrease how much money businesses pay for city services.

   b. The businesses will have to use solar and wind power.

6. The population of Manila is increasing quickly.

   a. The city will have to use electric buses and trains.

   b. The city will have to provide more housing.

Chant

GO ONLINE for the Chapter 5 Vocabulary & Grammar Chant

Writing Assignment

An essay about the causes of energy use

Scientists today are studying ways to meet energy needs in the future. In this assignment, you will look at ways that energy use is changing in your home, city, or country. You will examine the causes and make a recommendation for the future.

1. In the **introduction**, give background information about the place's energy needs. What kind of energy does it use? Are energy needs increasing or decreasing?

2. In the **support paragraphs**, explain why. Identify two different causes of the change in energy use. Consider issues in population, transportation, housing, or technology. Explain each cause. Give evidence from your own observations and experience.

3. In the **conclusion**, make recommendations for the future. What should be a priority for meeting the place's energy needs in the future?

Step 1 PREPARE

A. Read Julio's essay. What kind of energy use is increasing in Houston?

A Modern City

Houston, Texas, is a center of business for hospitals and oil companies. As a result, people from all over the world have moved to Houston for jobs in health and science. Because the population is growing, Houston's need for energy is increasing.

One cause is transportation. Today, many people live in homes outside the city. They need to drive to their jobs and other places. Because the city is getting bigger, people have to drive longer distances. As a result, they use more gas.

Another cause is housing. Today, Houstonians are buying bigger homes than they did in the past. These homes require more energy, especially during the hot summers. Also, people have more devices that require electricity. Most houses have at least one television and a computer, and homes with large families have several.

Houston will need more energy in the future, so the city will have to look for opportunities to save energy. First, Houston should provide more public transportation. Second, builders should build houses and office buildings that are more energy efficient.

B. Answer the questions about Julio's essay in Activity A. Write complete sentences.

1. Why is Houston's population growing?

_____

2. Why are Houston drivers using more gas?

_____

3. When do houses in Houston require more energy?

_____

4. Why do the houses require more energy?

_____

5. What recommendations for the future does the writer give?

_____

Writing Strategy

Writing an essay about causes

To explain a change, writers often analyze different causes. An essay about causes generally has the following parts.

The **introduction** states the topic and gives background information about the situation.

- A thesis statement states what is changing.
- It may use past, present, and/or perfect tenses.

The **support paragraphs** explain why the change is happening.

- The causes are usually in separate paragraphs.
- Transition words such as *because, so,* and *as a result* show relationships between causes and effects.
- It uses mainly present tenses.

The **conclusion** can explain how the writer feels about the situation.

- Writers often think about the causes and make recommendations for the future.
- Writers can use *could, should,* and *will have to* to give their recommendations.

GO ONLINE
for more
practice

C. Read the essay below. Choose the correct sentence from the box for each blank. Write it on the line.

> Second, Danish citizens are using less energy.
>
> I am proud of my country's energy goals for the future.
>
> ~~Denmark is a small country that has become a leader in clean energy.~~
>
> First, Denmark is getting a lot of electricity from wind.
>
> There are two main causes.

Denmark's Clean Energy

(a) _Denmark is a small country that has become a leader in clean energy._ The government, businesses, and citizens have worked together to help the environment and their country. As a result, Denmark's use of clean energy is increasing. (b) _____

_____

(c) _____
Denmark has a lot of open land, and the wind always blows, especially on the coast. The country has built large machines that collect energy from the wind. They send the energy to cities and homes. The wind is free, and the machines are helping the economy.

(d) _____
They buy energy-efficient devices for their homes, and they use solar power for electricity, especially during the day. Cities provide free bicycles, so many people do not need cars.

(e) _____
I think that Denmark should continue supporting clean energy. Also, the government could look for ways to make wind and solar energy even better.

A. Think about energy use in your home, city, or country. What kind of energy does the place use? What things are causing energy use to increase or decrease? Write your notes in the chart below. Then choose one for your Writing Assignment.

In my home	In my city	In my country

B. Read the parts of the Writing Assignment on page 82 again. Circle important words and phrases that help you organize your information. Then write notes about your topic for each section.

Introduction Start with background information about the place's energy needs. What kind of energy does it use? Are the energy needs increasing or decreasing?	

C. Circle the letter of the prepositional phrase that best completes each sentence. Then write it on the line.

1. There are still jobs in agriculture, especially *in small villages*   .

   a. in small villages

   b. in big cities

2. Biking to work is an option, especially _____.

   a. on sunny days

   b. on rainy days

3. We use heating devices, especially _____.

   a. during the summer

   b. during the winter

4. Energy needs have increased rapidly, especially _____.

   a. in the past ten years

   b. in the future

5. Solar energy is a good solution, especially _____.

   a. in cloudy regions

   b. in sunny regions

 D. Exchange essays with a partner. Ask and answer the questions below to help each other with ideas. Rewrite your essay.

Oxford 2000 🔑

Do you need more words to write about energy use? Use the Oxford 2000 list on page 133 to find more words for your essay.

Revising Questions

- What were your goals for the different parts of your essay?
- How can you use paragraphing skills to develop your ideas?
- Can you use *especially* to add a specific point about a time or place?
- Did you use Oxford 2000 words in your essay?

Step 5 EDIT

A. Read the paragraph. Find and correct six mistakes. The first mistake is corrected for you.

Changes in London

Today, special devices on London's sidewalks are ~~make~~ *making* energy from people's footsteps. Right now, the devices are produce electricity for lights at a local shopping center. However, scientists think that more public spaces could to use the devices. Especially in cities. Today, the technology expensive, so engineers will have find ways to make the devices more affordable. However, the footsteps will always be free!

 B. Read your essay again. Check (✓) the things in your essay.

Editing Checklist

○ 1. Capital letters, periods, and commas
○ 2. *could, should,* and *will have to*
○ 3. Present progressive to describe current trends
○ 4. *especially* with prepositional phrases

 C. Now write your final essay. Use the Editing Checklist to help you.

Step 6 PUBLISH

 Follow these steps to publish your paragraphs.

Publishing Steps

• Share your essay with a partner.

• Answer the questions.

  • Does the information about the place surprise you? Why or why not?

  • Do you have a different recommendation for the place?

• Put your essay in your portfolio!

Critical Thinking Question

Will it be difficult for people to adapt to clean energy in the future? Why or why not?

CHAPTER 6 Responding to Art

- Respond to ideas about future transportation solutions
- Use *would* and *would be able to*
- Make predictions and imagine solutions
- Practice using academic content in a short writing task

ACADEMIC CONTENT: Art that shows future transportation solutions

A. Ask and answer each question below with a partner.

1. What kinds of transportation have you used in the city? Check (✔) all that apply.

_____ a car   _____ a motorcycle   _____ an electric train

_____ a bicycle   _____ a public bus   _____ a subway

2. Read the statements below about public and private transportation. Circle *public* or *private* to show how you feel about each statement.

   a. *Public   Private*   transportation is cheaper.

   b. *Public   Private*   transportation is safer.

   c. *Public   Private*   transportation is more convenient.

   d. *Public   Private*   transportation uses less energy.

   e. *Public   Private*   transportation is good for the environment.

3. Which kind of transportation is a better solution for cities of the future? Why?

B. Look at the art below. How does each artist imagine the future?

Sky Trains

Flying Cars

C. Which picture from Activity B is a better solution for each statement below? Write *ST* for sky trains or *FC* for flying cars. Then discuss your answers with a partner.

_ST_ 1. I do not like looking for a parking place.

_____ 2. I like having time to text and play games.

_____ 3. I prefer to travel alone.

_____ 4. There are millions of people traveling in cities every day.

_____ 5. I want to get places fast, and I do not like waiting.

_____ 6. I don't like crowded trains and buses.

_____ 7. I need an affordable way to move around the city.

_____ 8. I like being in control of where I go.

PREWRITE

A. Read the Academic Writing Task below. Circle the words and phrases that give directions. Then use the Prewrite activities to plan your assignment.

ACADEMIC WRITING TASK Future transportation solutions

Cities must imagine solutions to meet the needs of the future. Which kind(s) of transportation do you think future cities need?

- First, make predictions about the transportation challenges that cities will face in the future. What will cause these challenges?

- Next, imagine which kind of transportation in the art on page 90 would solve these problems. Which one would be a better solution—sky trains or flying cars? Why?

B. What transportation challenges will cities face in the future? Circle the word in each sentence that matches your prediction. Then complete the sentence with a reason after *because*.

1. Streets will become (more) less crowded because there will be more cars.

2. Distances between places will *increase* *decrease* because _____

_____

3. *More* *Fewer* people will use public transportation because _____

_____

Critical Thinking
MAKING PREDICTIONS

When writers make predictions, they use evidence to draw conclusions about the future.

4. Cities will need to use *more* *less* space to build roads because _____

_____

5. There will be *more* *fewer* cars on city highways because _____

_____

6. There will be *more* *fewer* buildings because _____

_____

Language Focus

would and would be able to

Writers use *would (not)* + verb when they explain a future result. *Would* explains that the idea is imaginary or not real yet.

    *Flying cars **would be** different from traditional cars.*

    *Sky trains **would not travel** on the ground.*

Use *would be able to* + verb to explain a future ability that is imaginary or not real yet.

    *A flying car **would be able to fly** over traffic.*

    *On a sky train, people **would be able to see** interesting views of the city.*

GO ONLINE
for more
practice

C. **Complete each sentence that includes *would (not)* to explain the future results you imagine. Write *sky trains* or *flying cars* in the blank. Share your answers with a partner.**

1. _____Sky trains_____ would save space on the ground.

2. _____ would connect buildings in the city.

3. _____ would be a convenient way to travel.

4. _____ would not cause air pollution.

5. _____ would be expensive.

6. _____ would not move a large number of people.

7. _____ would need places to land.

8. _____ would reduce traffic on highways.

Critical Thinking

IMAGINING SOLUTIONS

When writers imagine solutions, they try to understand a problem first. Then they think of a solution that fits the problem.

D. Complete each sentence that includes _would (not) be able to_. Explain what you imagine.

1. Sky trains would be able to _fly above the streets._

2. Travelers on sky trains would be able to _____

3. Flying cars would be able to _____

4. Flying cars would not be able to _____

5. Drivers would be able to _____

WRITE AND EDIT

A. Use your sentences and ideas from Prewrite to write your assignment. Use the Academic Writing Task on page 91 to help guide your writing.

B. Use the checklist below to review your writing.

Academic Writing Task Checklist

Check (✓) for examples.

○ 1. I predicted transportation challenges that cities will face in the future.

○ 2. I explained why cities will face transportation challenges.

○ 3. I showed why sky trains or flying cars are a better solution.

○ 4. I used _would_ and _would be able to_ to explain imaginary situations.

○ 5. I used correct grammar, punctuation, and capitalization.

Chant

GO ONLINE
for the
Chapter 6
Vocabulary &
Grammar Chant

Look at the word bank for Unit 2. Check (✓) the words you know. Circle the words you want to learn better.

OXFORD 2000 🔑				
Adjectives	**Nouns**		**Verbs**	
bright	air	power	appear	increase
calm	appearance	priority	cause	produce
distant	citizen	rain	collect	provide
heavy	collection	region	crash	rain
rough	distance	star	disappear	reach
	electricity	surface	escape	require
	energy	top	fly	shine
	increase	tradition		
	machine	view		
	oil	wave		
	pollution			

PRACTICE WITH THE OXFORD 2000 🔑

A. Use the words in the chart. Match adjectives with nouns.

1. _____a bright star_____ 2. _____

3. _____ 4. _____

5. _____ 6. _____

B. Use the words in the chart. Match verbs with nouns.

1. _____produce electricity_____ 2. _____

3. _____ 4. _____

5. _____ 6. _____

C. Use the words in the chart. Match verbs with adjective noun partners.

1. _____fly to a distant region_____ 2. _____

3. _____ 4. _____

5. _____ 6. _____

GO ONLINE
for more
practice

UNIT 3 Media Studies

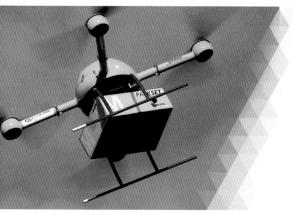

CHAPTER 7 How Can Celebrities Influence People?

- Use *which* and *which means that*
- Use *even though* and *even when*
- Write an essay about effects
- Refer to the names of people and organizations
- Write an effects essay about a media celebrity or organization

▲ VOCABULARY ▶ Oxford 2000 🔑 words to talk about people in the news

A. Write the letter of each group of sentences above the correct picture. Circle the boldfaced words you know. Discuss the words with a partner. Use a dictionary to help you with new words.

a.	b.
He is an Internet **celebrity** in the gaming world.	Inbee Park is a **professional** athlete who **competes** with golfers around the world.
Fans admire him because he finds new ways to win games.	She is a **positive role model** because she is polite and smart in **interviews**.

c.	d.
The organizers believe that there are **benefits** to camping in nature.	He believes that traveling can help create **peace** between countries.
They teach children how to **survive** in the wild.	He uses **media** to **influence** travelers to meet local people.

e.	f.
He **manages** a group of musicians by planning and organizing their shows.	Windri Widiesta Dahri designs clothes that **represent** her culture.
They **perform** at arts **events** in parks.	Many people **follow** her fashion **career online**.

1. _____

2. _____

3. _____

4. _____

travel = meeting local people
= peace between countries

5. _____

6. _____

B. Ask and answer each question with a partner. Try to use the target vocabulary.

1. What **media influences** you the most: social networking sites, news organizations, television shows, radio, or print media? Why?

2. What city landmark or natural landmark **represents** your country?

3. What are the health **benefits** of sports? Explain.

4. What **professional** actor, musician, or **athlete** would you like to **interview**, and what would you ask the person?

5. What do children learn when they **compete** in sports?

6. Who is a **celebrity** that is also a **role model**? Explain.

Oxford 2000 🔑

Use the Oxford 2000 list on page 133 to find more words to describe the pictures on these pages. Share your words with a partner.

WORD FORMS

These words can be used in different ways. Some nouns have two forms. The first is the person; the second is the concept.

Adjective	Noun	Verb	Adverb
athletic	athlete/athleticism		athletically
competitive	competition	compete	competitively
	performer/ performance	perform	
	interview	interview	
influential	influence	influence	
	manager/ management	manage	

C. Write each word from the first column before or after the words in the second to make phrases.

1. athletic   *athletic* club

2. survive   a dangerous situation

3. manager   an organized

4. interview   watch an

5. influence   young people

6. competition   between teams

D. Complete each set of sentences with the phrases from the box.

many interviews	interviews famous athletes

1. People watch his show because he _interviews famous athletes_.

2. There are _____ with celebrities online.

compete for money	entered a competition

3. Sometimes gamers become so good that they _____.

4. She became famous when she _____ at the age of five and won.

E. Use the words to describe each picture in two separate sentences.

1.
   a *competitive player / love competition*

   People like to watch a competitive player.

   The best players love competition.

   _____

2.
   a *talented athlete / athletic ability*

   _____

   _____

   _____

3.
   a *strong influence / an influential speaker*

   _____

   _____

   _____

4.
   a *powerful performance / perform together*

   _____

   _____

   _____

5.
   manage a kitchen / an organized manager

   _____

   _____

   _____

6.
   compete professionally / race competitively

   _____

   _____

   _____

GO ONLINE for more practice

GRAMMAR
▶ *which* and *which means that*
▶ *even though* and *even when*

A. Read Hana's essay. What are two things she likes about Inbee Park?

Korean Golfer Inbee Park

Inbee Park is a talented Korean golfer. She is in the news a lot because of her success, but it has not been easy for her. Sports media have made her famous, but being a famous golfer has had positive and negative effects.

Park's success has brought many benefits. She has won a lot of prize money, so she can drive an expensive car and travel around the world. She also has had opportunities to support other young golfers. She says that the golfer Se-Ri Pak influenced her to become a golfer, and now she wants to encourage other girls.

Park has also faced some challenges. Sometimes she has a bad day and loses. Then sports writers and photographers find her. They ask questions and take pictures, which means that many people will know about her loss. She smiles and stays positive even though she does not feel good at that moment.

The media can be good and bad for famous people, and young fans can learn from Park's example. She manages her image carefully at public events and smiles even when she loses. Park is also a good role model because she can have a bad day and then come back and win.

B. Circle the letter of the phrase that best completes each sentence about the essay in Activity A.

1. Park is a talented and successful golfer,

   a. which makes her popular in the media.

   b. which helps her with her education.

2. Park's success has given her the opportunity to be a role model for young fans,

   a. which means that she often loses.

   b. which means that she behaves politely in public.

3. Park sometimes gets media attention for playing badly,

   a. which means that she has to be strong and stay positive.

   b. which means that she likes the media.

Grammar Note

which and *which means that*

Sometimes writers want to add a comment that explains a whole sentence. They can do this by adding a comma and *which*.

> *When she loses, she does not get angry,* **which** *is a valuable life lesson for others.*

Which becomes the subject of the comment. It takes a singular verb.

> <u>*Visitors can go from her website to the store*</u>*,* **which** *makes it easy for people to shop online.*

> **which** is the subject that represents the whole sentence

Sometimes *which means that* is used to introduce a complete sentence.

> **new subject**

> *He just signed with the Los Angeles Galaxy,* **which means that** *people can see him in the media now.*

GO ONLINE
for more
practice

C. Combine the sentences with *which* or *which means that*.

1. He gives advice about saving money, _____ *which* _____ is helpful for families.

2. Building schools is the organization's main goal, _____ both workers and teachers can have jobs.

3. He gives an analysis of the game and posts video highlights, _____ helps people who have not seen the game.

4. She writes about changes in the downtown area, _____ people learn about things that affect them.

5. His online videos have helped a lot of people fix problems around their homes,

   _____ has made him popular with homeowners.

6. He gathers and posts articles about deep-sea exploration, _____ people who are interested in ocean science can learn about new developments in research.

D. Use the words in the chart to write sentences. Use correct punctuation.

The group is traveling and doing shows in different countries, which means that the world will learn more about its work.

Her mother was an actress She lived in Los Angeles She started acting when she was young	which	benefited her career gave her opportunities to learn about filmmaking was good because she learned about the movie business early
The group has posted videos A filmmaker is working on a movie about the group The group is traveling and doing shows in different countries	which means that	people can learn about performances and events the world will learn more about its work its influence will continue

Grammar Note

even though and *even when*

Writers use *even though* or *even when* to introduce information that is surprising, unexpected, or challenging. *Even though* and *even when* follow the punctuation rules for a complex sentence.

> When an *even though* clause comes before the main clause, it is followed by a comma.

Even though he lost the game, he had a smile on his face.

Even when it is raining, he practices.

> When an *even though* or *even when* clause follows the main clause, there is no comma.

She did not complain **even though** her arm was hurting.

They get up early to practice **even when** it is cold and dark outside.

GO ONLINE
for more
practice

E. Circle the letter of the phrase that best completes each sentence with *even though* or *even when*.

1. Hassan is very good at painting even though

   a. he does not see well.

   b. he is talented.

2. The organization Plant It Forward reached its goals even when

   a. it had good luck.

   b. it had problems.

3. The musicians in Playing for Change wrote songs together even though

   a. they did not speak the same language.

   b. they talked to each other a lot.

4. David Beckham is a famous soccer player even though

   a. he does not compete professionally anymore.

   b. a lot of people know about him.

5. People found Kahn's videos on the Internet even when

   a. he had a lot of media attention.

   b. he did not expect to be famous.

6. Jennifer Lawrence was a famous actress even when

   a. she became a celebrity.

   b. she was very young.

Chant

GO ONLINE
for the
Chapter 7
Vocabulary &
Grammar Chant

Writing Assignment

An effects essay about how a media celebrity or organization influences followers

Today, famous people easily influence the public through social and traditional media. In this assignment, you will look at the effects of this influence.

1. In the **introduction**, give background information about a media celebrity or organization that you admire. Who is the person or group? Where are they from? What are their goals?

2. In the **support paragraph(s)**, analyze the effects of that person or group on their public followers. Explain with details and examples.

3. In the **conclusion**, comment on how the person or group has used media. What do you learn about the power of the media to influence people?

Step 1 PREPARE

A. Read Tariq's essay. What does "Playing for Change" mean?

Playing for Change

Playing for Change is the name of a special group of musicians. They come from all over the world to play music together and work for peace. Many people like the group's goals. As a result, Playing for Change has grown into a successful organization that has had many positive effects.

People who listen to the music benefit from the experience. Even though they might not understand the language, they enjoy the songs and learn about the world's cultures. They see the band members having fun and working together, and they feel connected. Sometimes fans help with events by giving money or time.

Playing for Change also affects the people in the musicians' countries. The organization uses money from its performances to build schools and buy books and technology. Children develop academic skills and learn about traditional music, which makes them proud of themselves and their country.

Some people believe that social media have negative effects, but the musicians of Playing for Change show that media can have a positive influence. Their videos give people an opportunity to see musicians from distant places play music together, and their organization helps people to feel part of a bigger world.

B. Answer the questions to write summary sentences for the paragraphs in Activity A.

1. Who or what is Playing for Change?

_____

2. What is the first group that benefits from Playing for Change, and how?

_____

3. What is the second group that benefits from Playing for Change, and how?

_____

4. What lesson does the writer want to share about social media?

_____

Writing Strategy

Writing an essay about effects

Writers often organize papers to focus on the effects of a person's actions, a place, or an event.

The **introduction** states the topic and gives background information about the person, place, or event that causes the effects. A thesis statement connects the topic to the effects so that the organization is clear.

The **support paragraph(s)** introduce each effect with facts, explanations, and examples.

The **conclusion** comments on the topic by saying what the effects mean. It analyzes the changes that happen as a result of the effects, and it can make suggestions.

GO ONLINE
for more practice

C. Read the essay in Activity A again. Check (✓) the part of the essay that matches the writer's goal.

	Introduction	Support paragraphs	Conclusion
1. I decided to focus on the people who listen to the music in one paragraph because the readers might have experienced that benefit.			
2. To start, I wanted to introduce readers to Playing for Change and get them excited about the group's goal.			
3. I wanted readers to think about how social media can have a positive influence.			
4. Here I created a new paragraph because the group affects children's education differently from how the group affects regular fans.			

D. Read the paragraphs below. Number them in the correct order.

a. _____ Minecraft is an interesting but difficult game for new players, so they need a teacher. Paul Soares's videos introduce them to the game, so he has had a positive effect on helping the Minecraft community grow.

b. _____ Soares's work has also had a positive effect on education. Minecraft players can build historical buildings for a history project, or they can create the environment of a book for an English assignment using his ideas.

c. _____ Paul Soares, Jr., is a father, gamer, and professional in the online world of Minecraft, which is a building game. Players make gardens, farms, buildings, cities, mountains, oceans, and other environments. Soares has a positive effect on the community because he makes videos that teach new players how to survive.

d. _____ First, Soares's videos are valuable for children and their parents because they introduce new players to a game that is creative and builds community. When young players learn to grow food and work with others to build cities, they develop skills for the future.

A. Think about media celebrities and organizations that you admire. Who are the people or groups? Where are they from? What are their goals? Write your notes in the chart below. Then choose one for your Writing Assignment.

People or groups connected to sports or entertainment	Organizations that benefit people or society	Professionals who share information about an interest

B. Read the parts of the Writing Assignment on page 104 again. Circle important words and phrases that help you organize your information. Then write notes about your topic for each section.

Introduction Give background information about a media celebrity or organization that you admire. Who is the person or group? Where are they from? What are their goals?	
Support paragraph(s) Analyze the effects that the person or group has on public followers. Explain with details and examples. Do you want to use one or two paragraphs?	
Conclusion Comment on how the person or group has used media. What do you learn about the power of the media to influence culture?	

Step 3 WRITE

A. Look at your notes from Prewrite. Complete the sentences below about your topic. Then choose the ones you want to use for your background and topic sentences and thesis statement.

Word Partners

has had a positive effect on

negative effect

small effect

different effect

similar effect

GO ONLINE
to practice
word partners

Introduction Background sentences	…'s goal is to… … got started by…
Thesis statement	People admire… because… … has/have affected the public in many ways.
Support paragraph(s) Topic sentence(s)	… provides information about… Fans also learn about… … benefits people who…
Conclusion Concluding sentence	… has had an important effect on… … influences people in… ways.

 B. Write your essay. Use your notes and the Writing Assignment on page 104 to help guide your writing. Add a title.

Step 4 REVISE

A. Read Faten's essay. Why does she think fashion is important?

A Different Kind of Fashion Designer

Fashion is important because it shows people who you are. However, sometimes finding the right fashion is difficult. Windri Widiesta Dhari designs beautiful clothes for Muslim women. Dhari's company is called NurZahra, and its website and social media show her special approach to fashion.

One of Dhari's influences is nature. She uses colors that come from plants and trees. The colors are rich and deep, especially the blue of the indigo plant. In addition, she uses a Japanese method for making the colors.

Dhari also respects traditions. Local Indonesian women make the clothes using Indonesian methods. Dhari uses layers of material to create a look that represents Indonesia but is popular in other places. In fact, she had great success at Tokyo fashion week last year.

Dhari is a quiet but creative person. As a professional designer, she uses different social media to influence Muslim women to think about fashion choices, and she has started to influence the rest of the world as well.

B. Read the essay in Activity A again. Circle the person's name each time it is used.

Writing Strategy

Referring to the names of people and organizations
For people, introduce a person by his or her full name the first time. After that, use the person's last name.

> _Serena Williams_ is a tennis player. _Williams_ has influenced the sport a lot.

After they introduce an organization, writers can use an acronym (the first letter of each main word) in the rest of the essay.

> The _University of California, Los Angeles (UCLA)_ is a good choice for international students. Campus life at _UCLA_ is interesting.

GO ONLINE
for more practice

C. Write the correct form of the name of the person or organization in the blank.

1. The actress Emma Watson is now a goodwill ambassador for the United Nations (UN).

   _____ is a good person for this work because she is famous. Her

   popularity means that she can support the work of the _____.

2. The National Arab American Medical Association (NAAMA) has chapters in different

   cities. _____ supports educational, cultural, and social activities.

D. Exchange essays with a partner. Ask and answer the questions below to help each other with ideas. Rewrite your essay.

Oxford 2000 🔑

Do you need more words to write about media's influence? Use the Oxford 2000 list on page 133 to find more words for your essay.

Revising Questions

- What were your goals for the different parts of your essay?
- How can you use paragraphing skills to separate information from analysis of effects?
- Did you refer to people and/or organizations using the correct form?
- Did you use Oxford 2000 words in your essay?

Step 5 EDIT

A. Read the paragraphs. Find and correct seven mistakes. The first mistake is corrected for you.

World Traveler: Rick Steves

The travel writer Rick Steves's website is a good place to learn about the world. ~~Rick~~ *Steves* posts stories and pictures from his adventures. His goal is to influence travelers to connect with local people which can help them understand the world better.

Even though, he can afford expensive hotels, Rick Steves wants to help travelers save money. He provides information about family hotels and restaurants, which that means travelers and local people benefit. Rick sometimes suggests farms or homes, even when they are not as comfortable as regular hotels.

B. Read your essay again. Check (✓) the things in your essay.

Editing Checklist

○ 1. Capital letters, periods, and commas ○ 2. *which* and *which means that* to add a comment

○ 3. *even though* and *even when* ○ 4. Refer to the names of people and organizations

 C. Now write your final essay. Use the Editing Checklist to help you.

Step 6 PUBLISH

Follow these steps to publish your paragraphs.

Publishing Steps

- Share your essay with a partner.
- Answer the questions.
  - What did you know about the person or organization your partner wrote about?
  - Do you also admire the person or organization? Explain.
- Put your essay in your portfolio!

Critical Thinking Question

Do famous people have a responsibility to be good role models?

What Is an Issue in the News?

- Use adjective clauses with *where*
- Use *if* to talk about possibility
- Write a summary and a personal response
- Use *on the other hand*
- Write an essay about an issue in the news

▲ VOCABULARY ► Oxford 2000 🔑 words to talk about issues in the news

A. Write the letter of each group of sentences above the correct picture. Circle the boldfaced words you know. Discuss the words with a partner. Use a dictionary to help you with new words.

a. In the future, flying **robots** could **deliver packages** to people's homes. The robots could eventually **replace** workers who usually deliver the mail.	**b.** He can **access his bank account** using an app on his cell phone. The app shows his **personal information**, such as his name and account numbers.
c. The city has developed a new parking **system** for bicycles. Large devices **control** the bicycles when they go underground.	**d.** Ice climbing is an **extreme sport** that can put a person in dangerous **situations**. The climber wants to **avoid** getting an injury, so he uses **safety** equipment.
e. Safety is an **important issue** for the citizens, so the city has put cameras on busy sidewalks. Because of the cameras, **individuals** do not have **privacy** when they walk down the sidewalks.	**f.** People can read opinions from other **consumers** when they shop online. The glasses **protect** people's eyes from the sun.

1. _____

2. _____

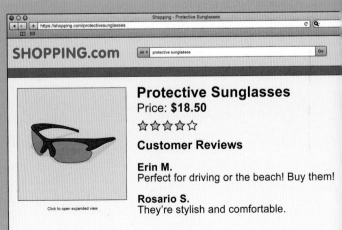

112   Unit 3 | Chapter 8

3. _____

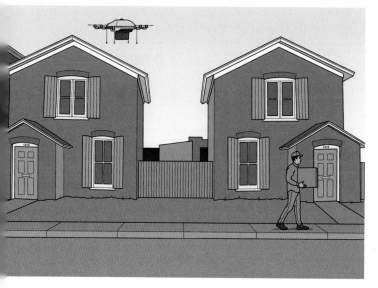

4. _____

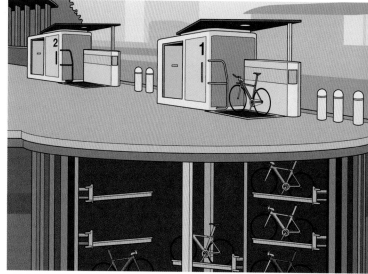

5. _____

6. _____

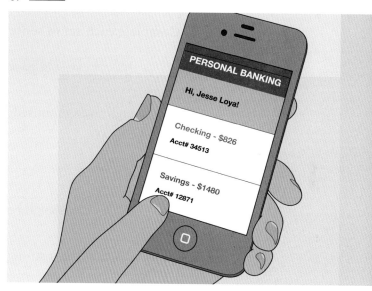

B. Ask and answer each question with a partner. Try to use the target vocabulary.

1. Can you name three sports that require **safety** equipment?

2. What jobs are **robots replacing** today? Why?

3. Can **individuals protect** themselves online? How?

4. Do you think businesses can **control** how **consumers** shop? Explain.

5. Where do you **access** the news?

6. What is **an important issue** in the news today? Why?

Oxford 2000 🔑

Use the Oxford 2000 list on page 133 to find more words to describe the pictures on these pages. Share your words with a partner.

WORD FORMS

Some verbs are formed by adding *-ize* to the adjective form.

Adjective	Noun	Verb	Adverb
accessible	access	access	
	delivery	deliver	
extreme			extremely
individual	individual	individualize	individually
personal	person	personalize	personally
private	privacy		privately
protective	protection	protect	
safe	safety		safely

C. **Complete each set of sentences with the phrases from the box.**

deliver packages	fast delivery

1. Even though I was promised _____ *fast delivery* _____, the package took three weeks to arrive.

2. Trucks _____ to homes and businesses.

personal beliefs	kind of person

3. My parents have had a strong influence on my _____.

4. She is the _____ who always helps others before herself.

need complete privacy	private information

5. Online banks protect people's _____ with special technology.

6. When I study, I _____ so that I can concentrate.

D. Use the words to describe each picture in two separate sentences.

1.

extremely difficult / extreme strength

Rock climbing is extremely difficult.

It requires extreme strength.

_____

2.

individual computers / work individually

_____

_____

_____

3.

accessible by car / have easy access to

_____

_____

_____

4.

wearing a safety helmet / keep his son safe

_____

_____

_____

5.

delivery person / personally delivered

_____

_____

_____

6.

protective clothing / needed for protection

_____

_____

_____

GO ONLINE
for more
practice

▲▲ GRAMMAR
► Adjective clauses with *where*
► *if* to talk about possibility

A. Read Sebastian's essay. Why is parkour an extreme sport?

Parkour in the Olympics

I recently read a story online about parkour and the Olympics. Parkour is an extreme sport. It is dangerous because people climb buildings without safety equipment. They also run across streets where there is a lot of traffic. Parkour started in France, but now people are doing it in other countries. Supporters of parkour want it to be an Olympic sport. However, so far they have not been successful because other people think that it is not a real sport.

I understand that there are two sides to this issue. If people race across city streets and climb buildings, it can be dangerous. Athletes can fall and get seriously hurt. Also, Olympic sports always have rules, but there are no rules for parkour yet.

On the other hand, if parkour is a competition, there can be rules and a clear winner. Parkour will still be dangerous, but there are already many dangerous sports in the Olympics. Over the years, the Olympics has added new sports because society has changed. I think that parkour could be attractive to young athletes and benefit the Olympics by keeping it current.

B. Check (✓) the picture that matches Sebastian's essay in Activity A.

Grammar Note

Adjective clauses with *where*

Writers often use adjective clauses with *where* to give more information about an online environment or a place in the real world.

*YouTube is a <u>website</u> **where people share videos.***
*Hollywood is a <u>place</u> **where many actors and filmmakers live.***
*They run across <u>streets</u> **where there is a lot of traffic.***

GO ONLINE
for more practice

C. Complete each sentence with a noun from the box + *where*.

city	hotel	street
country	museum	website

1. Google is a _____*website where*_____ people search for information online.

2. Tokyo is a _____ people can travel to work on high-speed trains.

3. Dubai has a _____ tourists stay in rooms below the ocean's surface.

4. I live on a peaceful _____ there is very little traffic.

5. New Zealand is a _____ people enjoy extreme sports.

6. The Louvre is a _____ there are many famous works of art.

D. Use the words in the chart to write sentences.

There are places where people can relax outside.

Facebook is a website		gamers create imaginary worlds
Minecraft is an online environment		individuals feel safe
The city is building parks	where	many fashion designers live
Paris is a city		neighbors enjoy helping each other
I live in a community		people post personal pictures
There are places		people can relax outside

Grammar Note

if to talk about possibility

Writers often use *if* when they want to describe a possible situation and result. Sentences with an *if* clause follow the punctuation rules for a complex sentence.

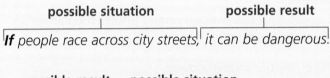

possible situation   possible result

If people race across city streets, it can be dangerous.

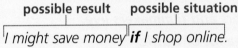

possible result   possible situation

I might save money if I shop online.

Writers use an *if* clause in the simple present to show possibility. Modal verbs such as *can* or *might* show possible results.

*If people **read** the news, they **can** learn about world events.*

*If the show **is** on television, I **might** watch it.*

GO ONLINE
for more
practice

E. Read each sentence. Underline the *if* clause. Add a comma when necessary.

1. <u>If photographers take pictures of celebrities</u>, they can sell them to newspapers.

2. If people try extreme sports they might get hurt.

3. Countries can feel proud if their athletes compete in the Olympics.

4. If companies want to improve a product they might ask consumers for their opinions.

5. If people go to museums they can learn about famous artists.

6. Football players can avoid injuries if they wear safety equipment.

F. Write the letter of the phrase on the right to complete each sentence on the left. Then rewrite the sentences below.

_b_ 1. Individuals can have problems   a. I might share it with my friends.

_____ 2. If I need a quiet place to study,   b. if they do not protect their information online.

_____ 3. If people admire a celebrity,   c. if you listen to radio news.

_____ 4. Countries can create more peace   d. they might follow him or her online.

_____ 5. You can hear interesting interviews   e. if they work together.

_____ 6. If I like a video on Facebook,   f. I can go to the library.

1. Individuals can have problems if they do not protect their information online.

2. _____

3. _____

4. _____

5. _____

6. _____

Chant

GO ONLINE
for the
Chapter 8
Vocabulary &
Grammar Chant

Writing Assignment

A summary and a personal response about an issue in the news

Today, people can choose news from newspapers, television, the radio, or online media. In this assignment, you will explain an issue in the media that you find interesting and then give your personal reaction to it.

1. First, summarize the issue using the questions *who? what? when? where? why?* and *how?* In your summary, focus only on facts from the news story and not your personal opinion.

2. Next, look at the issue from two different sides. What do different people want? What are the good and/or bad sides of the issue? Explain how you feel about the issue and the effects that it can have.

Step 1 PREPARE

A. Read Haiko's essay. How did Haiko learn about Amazon Prime Air?

Amazon Prime Air

I saw an interesting video on the Internet about Amazon Prime Air. Amazon.com wants to use flying robots to deliver packages. When you order something online, the company puts it in a box. A robot flies the box to your home, drops it at your front door, and then flies back to Amazon. The company's goal is to deliver packages to people in 30 minutes. Amazon believes that Prime Air will save time and money.

I think that some people will like Amazon Prime Air. We live in a world where customers expect quick delivery, so Prime Air will make them happy. On the other hand, there are some issues that I worry about. The robots could replace people. For example, if Amazon needs fewer delivery people, individuals might lose their jobs. I also think about safety. Robots that fly through the city might cause accidents. The technology behind Prime Air is exciting, but right now I think there are too many problems.

B. Answer the questions to write summary sentences for the paragraphs in Activity A.

1. How does Amazon Prime Air deliver packages?

_____

2. Why does Amazon want to use Prime Air?

_____

3. Does Haiko think that Amazon Prime Air is a good idea? Why or why not?

_____

Writing Strategy

Writing a summary and a personal response

Writers write a summary of a news story to retell the information in their own words. A summary does not include the writer's opinion. It generally has the following features.

- An introduction sentence states the topic and the source of the information (e.g., a newspaper, a video, the Internet).
- Sentences tell the main ideas of the story with facts about *who? what? when? where? why?* and *how?*

After a summary paragraph, writers can add personal response paragraphs that give their opinion about the issue. A personal response can include:

- Different opinions that people have about the issue
- Ideas that the writer likes or does not like

GO ONLINE
for more
practice

C. Read the summary sentences that explain a news story about bitcoins. Number the sentences in the correct order.

_____ a. Bitcoins are a new system of money that lets people pay for things with special computer files so that they do not have to use a bank.

_____ b. Then they can use them to buy plane tickets or food at restaurants.

_____ c. Bitcoins are a popular issue in the news right now.

_____ d. First, people buy bitcoins and save them on their computer.

D. Read the writer's personal response about bitcoins. Choose the correct sentence from the box for each blank. Write it on the line.

> Other people disagree with using bitcoins.
>
> I think they benefit consumers in two ways.
>
> I support bitcoins because they give individuals another choice.

My Thoughts on Bitcoins

I like bitcoins. (a)

First, people can save money because they do not pay bank charges. Also, bitcoins can help consumers keep their personal information private.

(b) _____

They do not like them because many businesses do not take them. On the other hand, consumers can still use cash or credit cards if they want.

(c) _____

_____

A. Think about issues in the news that you have learned about recently from the sources below. Write them in the chart. Then choose one for your Writing Assignment.

Social media	Radio or television	Newspapers and magazines

B. Read the parts of the Writing Assignment on page 120 again. Circle important words and phrases that help you organize your information. Then write notes about your topic for each section.

Summary paragraph Summarize the issue with information about *who, what, when, where, why,* and *how.* In your summary, focus only on facts from the news story, not your personal opinion.	
Personal response paragraph(s) Look at the issue from two different sides. What do different people want? What are the good and/ or bad sides of the issue? Explain how you feel about the issue and the effects that it can have. Do you want to use one or two paragraphs?	

Word Partners

personal
information

personal opinion

personal experience

personal
responsibility

personal safety

GO ONLINE
to practice
word partners

A. Look at your notes from Prewrite. Write the main sentences for your
introduction, support paragraphs, and conclusion. Use the phrases below or
write your own.

Summary paragraph Introduction sentence	I saw a video about… Recently, I read/heard a story about… … is a popular issue in the news right now.
Personal response paragraph(s) Introduction sentence(s)	I think that there are two sides to this issue. I think that some people… I (do not) like the idea of…

 B. Write your essay. Use your notes and the Writing Assignment on page 120 to
help guide your writing. Add a title.

Step 4 REVISE

A. Read Kayra's essay. How does she feel about cell phones in schools?

Cell Phones in Classrooms

Recently, I heard a story on the radio about cell phones in
American schools. In many high schools, students cannot use their
phones. On the other hand, there are some teachers who encourage cell
phones in class. For example, their students might search the Internet
if they need information for an assignment. There are also special
apps where students can take notes, access class assignments, and do
homework.

This issue has two sides. In some situations, teachers can lose
control of their students. For instance, students could use their phones to
text their friends or play games. On the other hand, I see many benefits.
For example, I think that students today learn better with technology.
Also, if they use their cell phones, they might be more excited about
learning. I think that schools should modernize and allow students to use
cell phones as they do in real life.

B. Read the essay in Activity A again. Circle *on the other hand.*

Writing Strategy

on the other hand

Writers use *on the other hand* when they want to introduce a sentence or paragraph with a contrasting situation or point of view. Put a comma after *on the other hand.*

> *Many consumers like the convenience of shopping online.* **On the other hand,** *some people think it is not safe.*

> *Amazon's robots will deliver packages quickly.* **On the other hand,** *there could be situations where the robots do not work correctly.*

GO ONLINE
for more
practice

C. Write the letter of the sentence on the right that correctly contrasts each sentence on the left. Then rewrite the sentences below with *on the other hand.*

____c____ 1. Parkour is dangerous.

_____ 2. Consumers value freedom.

_____ 3. YouTube videos can be useful.

_____ 4. I believe that buildings should be energy efficient.

_____ 5. I read about famous fashion designers.

_____ 6. Aisha Le is a famous celebrity.

On the other hand,

a. they also want control.

b. I have my own personal style.

c. it is exciting to watch.

d. she acts like a regular person.

e. I realize that they are expensive to build.

f. some give bad information.

1. Parkour is dangerous. On the other hand, it is exciting to watch.

2. _____

3. _____

4. _____

5. _____

6. _____

D. Exchange essays with a partner. Ask and answer the questions below to help each other with ideas. Rewrite your essay.

Oxford 2000 🔑

Do you need more words to write about issues in the news? Use the Oxford 2000 list on page 133 to find more words for your essay.

Revising Questions

- What were your goals for the different parts of your essay?
- How can you use paragraphing skills to develop your ideas?
- Can you use *on the other hand* to introduce a contrasting situation or point of view?
- Did you use Oxford 2000 words in your essay?

Step 5 EDIT

A. Read the essay. Find and correct eight mistakes. The first mistake is corrected for you.

Underground Bicycle Parking

watched
I ~~watch~~ an interesting video in school about bicycle parking in Tokyo, Japan. The city has develop a system that lets people store their bicycles underground. First, someone puts a bicycle into a special device on the sidewalk, then a robot takes the bicycle and parks it under the street. The system can keep 200 bicycle underground at the same time.

I think that underground parking for bikes is a good idea. Many people in Tokyo bike to work and school, on the other hand, they can experience problems because there are not enough parking spots on the sidewalks. If bikers use underground parking they do not have to worry about finding a spot. Another benefit is safety. Nobody can steal the bikes. If they are underground. Finally, the system provides more space for the millions of people who walk in the city which keeps the sidewalks less crowded. In my opinion, other big cities should use Tokyo's idea.

B. Read your essay again. Check (✓) the things in your essay.

Editing Checklist

- ○ 1. Capital letters, periods, and commas
- ○ 2. Adjective clauses with *where*
- ○ 3. *if* to talk about possibility
- ○ 4. *on the other hand*

C. Now write your final essay. Use the Editing Checklist to help you.

Step 6 PUBLISH

Follow these steps to publish your paragraphs.

Publishing Steps

- Share your essay with a partner.
- Answer the questions.
    - Is the issue important to you?
    - Which side of the issue do you agree with? Why?
- Put your essay in your portfolio!

Critical Thinking Question

What news media do you trust the most? Why?

CHAPTER 9 Applying Information from a Bar Graph

- Use evidence from a bar graph
- Report percentages
- Evaluate information
- Practice using academic content in a short writing task

ACADEMIC CONTENT: A bar graph showing social media behavior

A. How often do you use social media to do the following? Check (✓) your answers in the chart below.

	Never	Sometimes	Often	Always
1. share details about yourself				
2. communicate with friends or family				
3. post pictures				
4. watch videos				
5. share a news event				
6. comment on a news event				

B. The bar graph shows the results of a survey in which people answered questions about their use of social media. Are you similar to or different from most people in the survey? Discuss your answers with a partner.

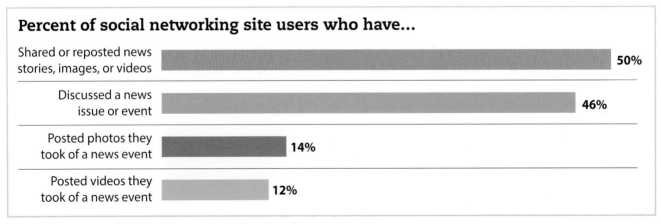

Percent of social networking site users who have...

Shared or reposted news stories, images, or videos — 50%

Discussed a news issue or event — 46%

Posted photos they took of a news event — 14%

Posted videos they took of a news event — 12%

Note: This question was asked of social networking site users who also get news online.
Source: Pew Research Center, phone survey Feb. 27–Mar. 2, 2014. Katerina Eva Matsa and Amy Mitchell. "8 Key Takeaways about Social Media and News." Pew Research Center, Washington, D.C. (March 26, 2014). http://www.journalism.org/2014/03/26/8-key-takeaways-about-social-media-and-news/, accessed October 17, 2014.

C. Fill in the chart with information from the bar graph in Activity B.

Percentage of social networking site users who have...	
shared or reposted a news story	
commented on a news story	
uploaded a photo of a news event	
uploaded a video of a news event	

PREWRITE

A. Read the Academic Writing Task below. Circle the words and phrases that give directions. Then use the Prewrite activities to plan your assignment.

ACADEMIC WRITING TASK Evaluate the role of social media

Some people believe that social media are not important. Others disagree. They say that people use them to learn and share important news. Use evidence from the survey bar graph on page 128 to draw your own conclusions. Write a short paper in which you answer the following questions.

- How does news travel in today's media? Do social networking sites play a role?

- What does the research show about the way people use social media to share news?

- What are the responsibilities of social networking users?

B. Check (✓) the statements that can be supported with evidence from the survey bar graph on page 128.

_____ 1. Social networking sites often help people learn about news events.

_____ 2. Social networking site users sometimes share opinions about news.

_____ 3. Social networking site users believe news that their friends post.

_____ 4. People often share news about sports and entertainment.

_____ 5. A few social networking site users also report on news events.

Critical Thinking
EVALUATING INFORMATION
People often evaluate evidence from research to form or possibly change an opinion.

Reporting percentages

When writing percentages, spell the number at the beginning of a sentence and when the number is below 10. Spell the word *percent* when you spell the number.

> **Thirty-seven percent** *of people click on a link because a friend recommended the news story.*
>
> *Only* **six percent** *of the population has never visited a social networking site.*

Write the number followed by the percent sign (%) when the percentage appears in the middle of a sentence and when the number is more than 10.

> *The report shows that* **70%** *of users click on links to news stories because they are interested in the topic.*

GO ONLINE
for more
practice

C. Circle the correct answer to complete each sentence.

1. *54%*   *Fifty-four percent* of social networking site users have never discussed a news event or issue.

2. The report shows that *50%*   *fifty percent* of users have shared or reposted news stories, images, or videos.

3. The report shows that *26%*   *twenty-six percent* of users have posted photos or videos they took of a news event.

4. *88%*   *Eighty-eight percent* of social networking site users have never uploaded a video of a news event.

D. Use information from the survey bar graph on page 128 to complete the sentences below.

1. Interestingly, _____46%_____ have discussed a news issue or event.

2. _____ have shared or reposted news stories, images, or videos.

3. The survey shows that _____ of users have posted a video of a news event.

4. _____ of social network site users have posted a photo of a news event.

5. The survey shows that _____ have never uploaded a photo.

E. Write supporting detail sentences using information from the survey bar graph on page 128.

1. Social networking sites are sources of news for some people. In fact, _____

_____

2. Social networking sites allow individuals to comment on news events. A survey

reported that _____

_____

3. Interestingly, regular people sometimes report news through social networking sites.

The survey shows that _____

_____

WRITE AND EDIT

A. Use your sentences and ideas from Prewrite to write your assignment. Use the Academic Writing Task on page 129 to help guide your writing.

B. Use the checklist below to review your writing.

Academic Writing Task Checklist

Check (✓) for examples.

○ 1. I explained how news travels in today's media.

○ 2. I wrote my opinion about the role of social networking in learning about and sharing news.

○ 3. I used research from the survey bar graph as evidence to support my conclusion.

○ 4. I reported percentages correctly.

○ 5. I drew conclusions about the responsibilities of social networking users.

○ 6. I used correct grammar, punctuation, and capitalization.

Chant

GO ONLINE
for the
Chapter 9
Vocabulary &
Grammar Chant

Look at the word bank for Unit 3. Check (✓) the words you know. Circle the words you want to learn better.

OXFORD 2000 🔑

Adjectives	Nouns		Verbs
extreme	account	package	admire
important	bank	peace	avoid
individual	benefit	performance	control
personal	career	person	deliver
positive	competition	protection	follow
private	event	safety	influence
professional	influence	situation	manage
safe	interview	sport	perform
	manager	system	protect
	model		replace
			represent
			survive

PRACTICE WITH THE OXFORD 2000 🔑

A. Use the words in the chart. Match adjectives with nouns.

1. _personal safety_   2. _____

3. _____   4. _____

5. _____   6. _____

B. Use the words in the chart. Match verbs with nouns.

1. _admire a performance_   2. _____

3. _____   4. _____

5. _____   6. _____

C. Use the words in the chart. Match verbs with adjective noun partners.

1. _follow an extreme sport_   2. _____

3. _____   4. _____

5. _____   6. _____

GO ONLINE
for more
practice

This is a list of the 2000 most important and useful words to learn at this stage in your language learning. These words have been carefully chosen by a group of language experts and experienced teachers, who have judged the words to be important and useful for three reasons.

- Words that are used very **frequently** (= very often) in English are included in this list. Frequency information has been gathered from the American English section of the Oxford English Corpus, which is a collection of written and spoken texts containing over 2 billion words.

- The keywords are frequent across a **range** of different types of text. This means that the keywords are often used in a variety of contexts, not just in newspapers or in scientific articles, for example.

- The list includes some important words which are very **familiar** to most users of English, even though they are not used very frequently. These include, for example, words which are useful for explaining what you mean when you do not know the exact word for something.

Names of people, places, etc. beginning with a capital letter are not included in the list of 2000 keywords. Keywords which are not included in the list are numbers, days of the week, and the months of the year.

A

a, an *indefinite article*
ability *n.*
able *adj.*
about *adv., prep.*
above *prep., adv.*
absolutely *adv.*
academic *adj.*
accept *v.*
acceptable *adj.*
accident *n.*
   by accident
according to *prep.*
account *n.*
accurate *adj.*
accuse *v.*
achieve *v.*
achievement *n.*
acid *n.*
across *adv., prep.*
act *n., v.*
action *n.*
active *adj.*
activity *n.*
actor, actress *n.*
actual *adj.*
actually *adv.*
add *v.*
address *n.*
admire *v.*
admit *v.*
adult *n.*
advanced *adj.*
advantage *n.*
adventure *n.*
advertisement *n.*
advice *n.*

advise *v.*
affect *v.*
afford *v.*
afraid *adj.*
after *prep., conj., adv.*
afternoon *n.*
afterward *adv.*
again *adv.*
against *prep.*
age *n.*
   aged *adj.*
ago *adv.*
agree *v.*
agreement *n.*
ahead *adv.*
aim *n., v.*
air *n.*
airplane *n.*
airport *n.*
alarm *n.*
alcohol *n.*
alcoholic *adj.*
alive *adj.*
all *adj., pron., adv.*
allow *v.*
all right *adj., adv.,*
   exclamation
almost *adv.*
alone *adj., adv.*
along *prep., adv.*
alphabet *n.*
already *adv.*
also *adv.*
although *conj.*
always *adv.*
among *prep.*
amount *n.*

amuse *v.*
analyze *v.*
analysis *n.*
ancient *adj.*
and *conj.*
anger *n.*
angle *n.*
angry *adj.*
animal *n.*
announce *v.*
another *adj., pron.*
answer *n., v.*
any *adj., pron., adv.*
anymore *(also* any more*)*
   adv.
anyone *(also* anybody*)*
   pron.
anything *pron.*
anyway *adv.*
anywhere *adv.*
apart *adv.*
apartment *n.*
apparently *adv.*
appear *v.*
appearance *n.*
apple *n.*
apply *v.*
appointment *n.*
appreciate *v.*
appropriate *adj.*
approve *v.*
area *n.*
argue *v.*
argument *n.*
arm *n.*
army *n.*
around *adv., prep.*

arrange *v.*
arrangement *n.*
arrest *v.*
arrive *v.*
arrow *n.*
art *n.*
article *n.*
artificial *adj.*
artist *n.*
artistic *adj.*
as *prep., conj.*
ashamed *adj.*
ask *v.*
asleep *adj.*
at *prep.*
atmosphere *n.*
atom *n.*
attach *v.*
attack *n., v.*
attention *n.*
attitude *n.*
attract *v.*
attractive *adj.*
aunt *n.*
authority *n.*
available *adj.*
average *adj., n.*
avoid *v.*
awake *adj.*
aware *adj.*
away *adv.*

B

baby *n.*
back *n., adj., adv.*
backward *adv.*
bad *adj.*

The Oxford 2000 List of Keywords

badly *adv.*
bag *n.*
bake *v.*
balance *n.*
ball *n.*
band *n.*
bank *n.*
bar *n.*
base *n., v.*
baseball *n.*
basic *adj.*
basis *n.*
bath *n.*
bathroom *n.*
be *v.*
beach *n.*
bear *v.*
beard *n.*
beat *v.*
beautiful *adj.*
beauty *n.*
because *conj.*
become *v.*
bed *n.*
bedroom *n.*
beer *n.*
before *prep., conj., adv.*
begin *v.*
beginning *n.*
behave *v.*
behavior *n.*
behind *prep., adv.*
belief *n.*
believe *v.*
bell *n.*
belong *v.*
below *prep., adv.*
belt *n.*
bend *v.*
benefit *n.*
beside *prep.*
best *adj., adv., n.*
better *adj., adv.*
between *prep., adv.*
beyond *prep., adv.*
bicycle *n.*
big *adj.*
bill *n.*
bird *n.*
birth *n.*
birthday *n.*
bite *v.*
bitter *adj.*
black *adj.*
blame *v.*
block *n.*
blood *n.*
blow *v., n.*
blue *adj., n.*

board *n.*
boat *n.*
body *n.*
boil *v.*
bomb *n., v.*
bone *n.*
book *n.*
boot *n.*
border *n.*
bored *adj.*
boring *adj.*
born: be born *v.*
borrow *v.*
boss *n.*
both *adj., pron.*
bother *v.*
bottle *n.*
bottom *n.*
bowl *n.*
box *n.*
boy *n.*
boyfriend *n.*
brain *n.*
branch *n.*
brave *adj.*
bread *n.*
break *v.*
breakfast *n.*
breath *n.*
breathe *v.*
brick *n.*
bridge *n.*
brief *adj.*
bright *adj.*
bring *v.*
broken *adj.*
brother *n.*
brown *adj., n.*
brush *n., v.*
bubble *n.*
build *v.*
building *n.*
bullet *n.*
burn *v.*
burst *v.*
bury *v.*
bus *n.*
bush *n.*
business *n.*
busy *adj.*
but *conj.*
butter *n.*
button *n.*
buy *v.*
by *prep.*
bye *exclamation*

C

cabinet *n.*

cake *n.*
calculate *v.*
call *v., n.*
calm *adj.*
camera *n.*
camp *n., v.*
can *modal v., n.*
cancel *v.*
candy *n.*
capable *adj.*
capital *n.*
car *n.*
card *n.*
care *n., v.*
   take care of
   care for
career *n.*
careful *adj.*
carefully *adv.*
careless *adj.*
carelessly *adv.*
carry *v.*
case *n.*
   in case (of)
cash *n.*
cat *n.*
catch *v.*
cause *n., v.*
CD *n.*
ceiling *n.*
celebrate *v.*
cell *n.*
cell phone *n.*
cent *n.*
center *n.*
centimeter *n.*
central *adj.*
century *n.*
ceremony *n.*
certain *adj.*
certainly *adv.*
chain *n., v.*
chair *n.*
challenge *n.*
chance *n.*
change *v., n.*
character *n.*
characteristic *n.*
charge *n., v.*
charity *n.*
chase *v., n.*
cheap *adj.*
cheat *v.*
check *v., n.*
cheek *n.*
cheese *n.*
chemical *adj., n.*
chemistry *n.*
chest *n.*

chicken *n.*
chief *adj., n.*
child *n.*
childhood *n.*
chin *n.*
chocolate *n.*
choice *n.*
choose *v.*
church *n.*
cigarette *n.*
circle *n.*
citizen *n.*
city *n.*
class *n.*
clean *adj., v.*
clear *adj., v.*
clearly *adv.*
climate *n.*
climb *v.*
clock *n.*
close /kloʊs/ *adj., adv.*
close /kloʊz/ *v.*
closed *adj.*
cloth *n.*
clothes *n.*
clothing *n.*
cloud *n.*
club *n.*
coast *n.*
coat *n.*
coffee *n.*
coin *n.*
cold *adj., n.*
collect *v.*
collection *n.*
college *n.*
color *n., v.*
column *n.*
combination *n.*
combine *v.*
come *v.*
comfortable *adj.*
command *n.*
comment *n., v.*
common *adj.*
communicate *v.*
communication *n.*
community *n.*
company *n.*
compare *v.*
comparison *n.*
competition *n.*
complain *v.*
complaint *n.*
complete *adj.*
completely *adv.*
complicated *adj.*
computer *n.*
concentrate *v.*

concert *n.*
conclusion *n.*
condition *n.*
confidence *n.*
confident *adj.*
confuse *v.*
confused *adj.*
connect *v.*
connection *n.*
conscious *adj.*
consider *v.*
consist *v.*
constant *adj.*
contact *n., v.*
contain *v.*
container *n.*
continent *n.*
continue *v.*
continuous *adj.*
contract *n.*
contrast *n.*
contribute *v.*
control *n., v.*
convenient *adj.*
conversation *n.*
convince *v.*
cook *v.*
cookie *n.*
cooking *n.*
cool *adj.*
copy *n., v.*
corner *n.*
correct *adj., v.*
correctly *adv.*
cost *n., v.*
cotton *n.*
cough *v.*
could *modal v.*
count *v.*
country *n.*
county *n.*
couple *n.*
course *n.*
   of course
court *n.*
cousin *n.*
cover *v., n.*
covering *n.*
cow *n.*
crack *v.*
crash *n., v.*
crazy *adj.*
cream *n., adj.*
create *v.*
credit card *n.*
crime *n.*
criminal *adj., n.*
crisis *n.*
criticism *n.*

criticize *v.*
cross *v.*
crowd *n.*
cruel *adj.*
crush *v.*
cry *v.*
culture *n.*
cup *n.*
curly *adj.*
curve *n.*
curved *adj.*
custom *n.*
customer *n.*
cut *v., n.*

D
dad *n.*
damage *n., v.*
dance *n., v.*
dancer *n.*
danger *n.*
dangerous *adj.*
dark *adj., n.*
date *n.*
daughter *n.*
day *n.*
dead *adj.*
deal *v.*
dear *adj.*
death *n.*
debt *n.*
decide *v.*
decision *n.*
decorate *v.*
deep *adj.*
deeply *adv.*
defeat *v.*
definite *adj.*
definitely *adv.*
definition *n.*
degree *n.*
deliberately *adv.*
deliver *v.*
demand *n., v.*
dentist *n.*
deny *v.*
department *n.*
depend *v.*
depression *n.*
describe *v.*
description *n.*
desert *n.*
deserve *v.*
design *n., v.*
desk *n.*
despite *prep.*
destroy *v.*
detail *n.*
   in detail

determination *n.*
determined *adj.*
develop *v.*
development *n.*
device *n.*
diagram *n.*
dictionary *n.*
die *v.*
difference *n.*
different *adj.*
difficult *adj.*
difficulty *n.*
dig *v.*
dinner *n.*
direct *adj., adv., v.*
direction *n.*
directly *adv.*
dirt *n.*
dirty *adj.*
disadvantage *n.*
disagree *v.*
disagreement *n.*
disappear *v.*
disappoint *v.*
disaster *n.*
discover *v.*
discuss *v.*
discussion *n.*
disease *n.*
disgusting *adj.*
dish *n.*
dishonest *adj.*
disk *n.*
distance *n.*
distant *adj.*
disturb *v.*
divide *v.*
division *n.*
divorce *n., v.*
do *v., auxiliary v.*
doctor *n. (abbr.* Dr.*)*
document *n.*
dog *n.*
dollar *n.*
door *n.*
dot *n.*
double *adj.*
doubt *n.*
down *adv., prep.*
downstairs *adv., adj.*
downward *adv.*
draw *v.*
drawer *n.*
drawing *n.*
dream *n., v.*
dress *n., v.*
drink *n., v.*
drive *v., n.*
driver *n.*

drop *v., n.*
drug *n.*
dry *adj., v.*
during *prep.*
dust *n.*
duty *n.*
DVD *n.*

E
each *adj., pron.*
each other *pron.*
ear *n.*
early *adj., adv.*
earn *v.*
earth *n.*
easily *adv.*
east *n., adj., adv.*
eastern *adj.*
easy *adj.*
eat *v.*
economic *adj.*
economy *n.*
edge *n.*
educate *v.*
education *n.*
effect *n.*
effort *n.*
e.g. *abbr.*
egg *n.*
either *adj., pron., adv.*
election *n.*
electric *adj.*
electrical *adj.*
electricity *n.*
electronic *adj.*
else *adv.*
e-mail *(also* email*) n., v.*
embarrass *v.*
embarrassed *adj.*
emergency *n.*
emotion *n.*
employ *v.*
employment *n.*
empty *adj.*
encourage *v.*
end *n., v.*
   in the end
enemy *n.*
energy *n.*
engine *n.*
enjoy *v.*
enjoyable *adj.*
enjoyment *n.*
enough *adj., pron., adv.*
enter *v.*
entertain *v.*
entertainment *n.*
enthusiasm *n.*
enthusiastic *adj.*

entrance *n.*
environment *n.*
equal *adj.*
equipment *n.*
error *n.*
escape *v.*
especially *adv.*
essential *adj.*
etc. *abbr.*
even *adv.*
evening *n.*
event *n.*
ever *adv.*
every *adj.*
everybody *pron.*
everyone *pron.*
everything *pron.*
everywhere *adv.*
evidence *n.*
evil *adj.*
exact *adj.*
exactly *adv.*
exaggerate *v.*
exam *n.*
examination *n.*
examine *v.*
example *n.*
excellent *adj.*
except *prep.*
exchange *v., n.*
excited *adj.*
excitement *n.*
exciting *adj.*
excuse *n., v.*
exercise *n.*
exist *v.*
exit *n.*
expect *v.*
expensive *adj.*
experience *n., v.*
experiment *n.*
expert *n.*
explain *v.*
explanation *n.*
explode *v.*
explore *v.*
explosion *n.*
expression *n.*
extra *adj., adv.*
extreme *adj.*
extremely *adv.*
eye *n.*

F
face *n., v.*
fact *n.*
factory *n.*
fail *v.*
failure *n.*

fair *adj.*
fall *v., n.*
false *adj.*
familiar *adj.*
family *n.*
famous *adj.*
far *adv., adj.*
farm *n.*
farmer *n.*
fashion *n.*
fashionable *adj.*
fast *adj., adv.*
fasten *v.*
fat *adj., n.*
father *n.*
fault *n.*
favor *n.*
   in favor
favorite *adj., n.*
fear *n., v.*
feather *n.*
feature *n.*
feed *v.*
feel *v.*
feeling *n.*
female *adj.*
fence *n.*
festival *n.*
few *adj., pron.*
   a few
field *n.*
fight *v., n.*
figure *n.*
file *n.*
fill *v.*
film *n.*
final *adj.*
finally *adv.*
financial *adj.*
find *v.*
   find out sth
fine *adj.*
finger *n.*
finish *v.*
fire *n., v.*
firm *n., adj.*
firmly *adv.*
first *adj., adv., n.*
   at first
fish *n.*
fit *v., adj.*
fix *v.*
fixed *adj.*
flag *n.*
flame *n.*
flash *v.*
flat *adj.*
flavor *n.*
flight *n.*

float *v.*
flood *n.*
floor *n.*
flour *n.*
flow *v.*
flower *n.*
fly *v.*
fold *v.*
follow *v.*
food *n.*
foot *n.*
football *n.*
for *prep.*
force *n., v.*
foreign *adj.*
forest *n.*
forever *adv.*
forget *v.*
forgive *v.*
fork *n.*
form *n., v.*
formal *adj.*
forward *adv.*
frame *n.*
free *adj., v., adv.*
freedom *n.*
freeze *v.*
fresh *adj.*
friend *n.*
friendly *adj.*
friendship *n.*
frighten *v.*
from *prep.*
front *n., adj.*
   in front
frozen *adj.*
fruit *n.*
fry *v.*
fuel *n.*
full *adj.*
fully *adv.*
fun *n., adj.*
funny *adj.*
fur *n.*
furniture *n.*
further *adj., adv.*
future *n., adj.*

G
gain *v.*
gallon *n.*
game *n.*
garbage *n.*
garden *n.*
gas *n.*
gate *n.*
general *adj.*
   in general
generally *adv.*

generous *adj.*
gentle *adj.*
gently *adv.*
gentleman *n.*
get *v.*
gift *n.*
girl *n.*
girlfriend *n.*
give *v.*
glass *n.*
glasses *n.*
global *adj.*
glove *n.*
go *v.*
goal *n.*
god *n.*
gold *n., adj.*
good *adj., n.*
goodbye *exclamation*
goods *n.*
govern *v.*
government *n.*
grade *n., v.*
grain *n.*
gram *n.*
grammar *n.*
grandchild *n.*
grandfather *n.*
grandmother *n.*
grandparent *n.*
grass *n.*
grateful *adj.*
gray *adj., n.*
great *adj.*
green *adj., n.*
groceries *n.*
ground *n.*
group *n.*
grow *v.*
growth *n.*
guard *n., v.*
guess *v.*
guest *n.*
guide *n.*
guilty *adj.*
gun *n.*

H
habit *n.*
hair *n.*
half *n., adj., pron., adv.*
hall *n.*
hammer *n.*
hand *n.*
handle *v., n.*
hang *v.*
happen *v.*
happiness *n.*
happy *adj.*

hard *adj., adv.*
hardly *adv.*
harm *n., v.*
harmful *adj.*
hat *n.*
hate *v., n.*
have *v.*
    have to *modal v.*
he *pron.*
head *n.*
health *n.*
healthy *adj.*
hear *v.*
heart *n.*
heat *n., v.*
heavy *adj.*
height *n.*
hello *exclamation*
help *v., n.*
helpful *adj.*
her *pron., adj.*
here *adv.*
hers *pron.*
herself *pron.*
hide *v.*
high *adj., adv.*
highly *adv.*
high school *n.*
highway *n.*
hill *n.*
him *pron.*
himself *pron.*
hire *v.*
his *adj., pron.*
history *n.*
hit *v., n.*
hold *v., n.*
hole *n.*
holiday *n.*
home *n., adv..*
honest *adj.*
hook *n.*
hope *v., n.*
horn *n.*
horse *n.*
hospital *n.*
hot *adj.*
hotel *n.*
hour *n.*
house *n.*
how *adv.*
however *adv.*
huge *adj.*
human *adj., n.*
humor *n.*
hungry *adj.*
hunt *v.*
hurry *v., n.*
hurt *v.*

husband *n.*

I
I *pron.*
ice *n.*
idea *n.*
identify *v.*
if *conj.*
ignore *v.*
illegal *adj.*
illegally *adv.*
illness *n.*
image *n.*
imagination *n.*
imagine *v.*
immediate *adj.*
immediately *adv.*
impatient *adj.*
importance *n.*
important *adj.*
impossible *adj.*
impress *v.*
impression *n.*
improve *v.*
improvement *n.*
in *prep., adv.*
inch *n.*
include *v.*
including *prep.*
increase *v., n.*
indeed *adv.*
independent *adj.*
individual *adj.*
industry *n.*
infection *n.*
influence *n.*
inform *v.*
informal *adj.*
information *n.*
injure *v.*
injury *n.*
insect *n.*
inside *prep., adv., n., adj.*
instead *adv., prep.*
instruction *n.*
instrument *n.*
insult *v., n.*
intelligent *adj.*
intend *v.*
intention *n.*
interest *n., v.*
interested *adj.*
interesting *adj.*
international *adj.*
Internet *n.*
interrupt *v.*
interview *n.*
into *prep.*
introduce *v.*

introduction *n.*
invent *v.*
investigate *v.*
invitation *n.*
invite *v.*
involve *v.*
iron *n.*
island *n.*
issue *n.*
it *pron.*
item *n.*
its *adj.*
itself *pron.*

J
jacket *n.*
jeans *n.*
jewelry *n.*
job *n.*
join *v.*
joke *n., v.*
judge *n., v.*
judgment (*also*
    judgement) *n.*
juice *n.*
jump *v.*
just *adv.*

K
keep *v.*
key *n.*
kick *v., n.*
kid *n., v.*
kill *v.*
kilogram (*also* kilo) *n.*
kilometer *n.*
kind *n., adj.*
kindness *n.*
king *n.*
kiss *v., n.*
kitchen *n.*
knee *n.*
knife *n.*
knock *v., n.*
knot *n.*
know *v.*
knowledge *n.*

L
lack *n.*
lady *n.*
lake *n.*
lamp *n.*
land *n., v.*
language *n.*
large *adj.*
last *adj., adv., n., v.*
late *adj., adv.*
later *adv.*

laugh *v.*
laundry *n.*
law *n.*
lawyer *n.*
lay *v.*
layer *n.*
lazy *adj.*
lead /lid/ *v.*
leader *n.*
leaf *n.*
lean *v.*
learn *v.*
least *adj., pron., adv.*
    at least
leather *n.*
leave *v.*
left *adj., adv., n.*
leg *n.*
legal *adj.*
legally *adv.*
lemon *n.*
lend *v.*
length *n.*
less *adj., pron., adv.*
lesson *n.*
let *v.*
letter *n.*
level *n.*
library *n.*
lid *n.*
lie *v., n.*
life *n.*
lift *v.*
light *n., adj., v.*
lightly *adv.*
like *prep., v., conj.*
likely *adj.*
limit *n., v.*
line *n.*
lip *n.*
liquid *n., adj.*
list *n., v.*
listen *v.*
liter *n.*
literature *n.*
little *adj., pron., adv.*
a little
live /lɪv/ *v.*
living *adj.*
load *n., v.*
loan *n.*
local *adj.*
lock *v., n.*
lonely *adj.*
long *adj., adv.*
look *v., n.*
loose *adj.*
lose *v.*
loss *n.*

The Oxford 2000 List of Keywords

lost *adj.*
lot *pron., adv.*
  a lot (of)
  lots (of)
loud *adj.*
loudly *adv.*
love *n., v.*
low *adj., adv.*
luck *n.*
lucky *adj.*
lump *n.*
lunch *n.*

M
machine *n.*
magazine *n.*
magic *n., adj.*
mail *n., v.*
main *adj.*
mainly *adv.*
make *v.*
male *adj., n.*
man *n.*
manage *v.*
manager *n.*
many *adj., pron.*
map *n.*
mark *n., v.*
market *n.*
marriage *n.*
married *adj.*
marry *v.*
match *n., v.*
material *n.*
math *n.*
mathematics *n.*
matter *n., v.*
may *modal v.*
maybe *adv.*
me *pron.*
meal *n.*
mean *v.*
meaning *n.*
measure *v., n.*
measurement *n.*
meat *n.*
medical *adj.*
medicine *n.*
medium *adj.*
meet *v.*
meeting *n.*
melt *v.*
member *n.*
memory *n.*
mental *adj.*
mention *v.*
mess *n.*
message *n.*
messy *adj.*

metal *n.*
method *n.*
meter *n.*
middle *n., adj.*
midnight *n.*
might *modal v.*
mile *n.*
milk *n.*
mind *n., v.*
mine *pron.*
minute *n.*
mirror *n.*
Miss *n.*
miss *v.*
missing *adj.*
mistake *n.*
mix *v.*
mixture *n.*
model *n.*
modern *adj.*
mom *n.*
moment *n.*
money *n.*
month *n.*
mood *n.*
moon *n.*
moral *adj.*
morally *adv.*
more *adj., pron., adv.*
morning *n.*
most *adj., pron., adv.*
mostly *adv.*
mother *n.*
motorcycle *n.*
mountain *n.*
mouse *n.*
mouth *n.*
move *v., n.*
movement *n.*
movie *n.*
Mr. *abbr.*
Mrs. *abbr.*
Ms. *abbr.*
much *adj., pron., adv.*
mud *n.*
multiply *v.*
murder *n., v.*
muscle *n.*
museum *n.*
music *n.*
musical *adj.*
musician *n.*
must *modal v.*
my *adj.*
myself *pron.*
mysterious *adj.*

N
nail *n.*

name *n., v.*
narrow *adj.*
nation *n.*
national *adj.*
natural *adj.*
nature *n.*
navy *n.*
near *adj., adv., prep.*
nearby *adj., adv.*
nearly *adv.*
neat *adj.*
neatly *adv.*
necessary *adj.*
neck *n.*
need *v., n.*
needle *n.*
negative *adj.*
neighbor *n.*
neither *adj., pron., adv.*
nerve *n.*
nervous *adj.*
net *n.*
never *adv.*
new *adj.*
news *n.*
newspaper *n.*
next *adj., adv., n.*
nice *adj.*
night *n.*
no *exclamation, adj.*
nobody *pron.*
noise *n.*
noisy *adj.*
noisily *adv.*
none *pron.*
nonsense *n.*
no one *pron.*
nor *conj.*
normal *adj.*
normally *adv.*
north *n., adj., adv.*
northern *adj.*
nose *n.*
not *adv.*
note *n.*
nothing *pron.*
notice *v.*
novel *n.*
now *adv.*
nowhere *adv.*
nuclear *adj.*
number (*abbr.* No., no.) *n.*
nurse *n.*
nut *n.*

O
object *n.*
obtain *v.*
obvious *adj.*

occasion *n.*
occur *v.*
ocean *n.*
o'clock *adv.*
odd *adj.*
of *prep.*
off *adv., prep.*
offense *n.*
offer *v., n.*
office *n.*
officer *n.*
official *adj., n.*
officially *adv.*
often *adv.*
oh *exclamation*
oil *n.*
OK (*also* okay)
  exclamation, adj., adv.
old *adj.*
old-fashioned *adj.*
on *prep., adv.*
once *adv., conj.*
one *number, adj., pron.*
onion *n.*
only *adj., adv.*
onto *prep.*
open *adj., v.*
operate *v.*
operation *n.*
opinion *n.*
opportunity *n.*
opposite *adj., adv., n., prep.*
or *conj.*
orange *n., adj.*
order *n., v.*
ordinary *adj.*
organization *n.*
organize *v.*
organized *adj.*
original *adj., n.*
other *adj., pron.*
otherwise *adv.*
ought to *modal v.*
ounce *n.*
our *adj.*
ours *pron.*
ourselves *pron.*
out *adj., adv.*
out of *prep.*
outside *n., adj., prep., adv.*
oven *n.*
over *adv., prep.*
owe *v.*
own *adj., pron., v.*
owner *n.*

P
pack *v., n.*
package *n.*

page *n.*
pain *n.*
painful *adj.*
paint *n., v.*
painter *n.*
painting *n.*
pair *n.*
pale *adj.*
pan *n.*
pants *n.*
paper *n.*
parent *n.*
park *n., v.*
part *n.*
   take part (in)
particular *adj.*
particularly *adv.*
partly *adv.*
partner *n.*
party *n.*
pass *v.*
passage *n.*
passenger *n.*
passport *n.*
past *adj., n., prep., adv.*
path *n.*
patient *n., adj.*
pattern *n.*
pause *v.*
pay *v., n.*
payment *n.*
peace *n.*
peaceful *adj.*
pen *n.*
pencil *n.*
people *n.*
perfect *adj.*
perform *v.*
performance *n.*
perhaps *adv.*
period *n.*
permanent *adj.*
permission *n.*
person *n.*
personal *adj.*
personality *n.*
persuade *v.*
pet *n.*
phone *n.*
photo *n.*
photograph *n.*
phrase *n.*
physical *adj.*
physically *adv.*
piano *n.*
pick *v.*
   pick sth up
picture *n.*
piece *n.*

pig *n.*
pile *n.*
pilot *n.*
pin *n.*
pink *adj., n.*
pint *n.*
pipe *n.*
place *n., v.*
   take place
plain *adj.*
plan *n., v.*
plane *n.*
planet *n.*
plant *n., v.*
plastic *n.*
plate *n.*
play *v., n.*
player *n.*
pleasant *adj.*
please *exclamation, v.*
pleased *adj.*
pleasure *n.*
plenty *pron.*
pocket *n.*
poem *n.*
poetry *n.*
point *n., v.*
pointed *adj.*
poison *n., v.*
poisonous *adj.*
police *n.*
polite *adj.*
politely *adv.*
political *adj.*
politician *n.*
politics *n.*
pollution *n.*
pool *n.*
poor *adj.*
popular *adj.*
port *n.*
position *n.*
positive *adj.*
possibility *n.*
possible *adj.*
possibly *adv.*
post *n.*
pot *n.*
potato *n.*
pound *n.*
pour *v.*
powder *n.*
power *n.*
powerful *adj.*
practical *adj.*
practice *n., v.*
prayer *n.*
prefer *v.*
pregnant *adj.*

preparation *n.*
prepare *v.*
present *adj., n., v.*
president *n.*
press *n., v.*
pressure *n.*
pretend *v.*
pretty *adv., adj.*
prevent *v.*
previous *adj.*
price *n.*
priest *n.*
principal *n.*
print *v.*
priority *n.*
prison *n.*
prisoner *n.*
private *adj.*
prize *n.*
probable *adj.*
probably *adv.*
problem *n.*
process *n.*
produce *v.*
product *n.*
production *n.*
professional *adj.*
profit *n.*
program *n.*
progress *n.*
project *n.*
promise *v., n.*
pronunciation *n.*
proof *n.*
proper *adj.*
property *n.*
protect *v.*
protection *n.*
protest *n.*
proud *adj.*
prove *v.*
provide *v.*
public *adj., n.*
   publicly *adv.*
publish *v.*
pull *v.*
punish *v.*
punishment *n.*
pure *adj.*
purple *adj., n.*
purpose *n.*
   on purpose
push *v., n.*
put *v.*

Q
quality *n.*
quantity *n.*
quarter *n.*

queen *n.*
question *n., v.*
quick *adj.*
quickly *adv.*
quiet *adj.*
quietly *adv.*
quite *adv.*

R
race *n., v.*
radio *n.*
railroad *n.*
rain *n., v.*
raise *v.*
rare *adj.*
rarely *adv.*
rate *n.*
rather *adv.*
reach *v.*
reaction *n.*
read *v.*
ready *adj.*
real *adj.*
reality *n.*
realize *v.*
really *adv.*
reason *n.*
reasonable *adj.*
receive *v.*
recent *adj.*
recently *adv.*
recognize *v.*
recommend *v.*
record *n., v.*
recover *v.*
red *adj., n.*
reduce *v.*
refer to *v.*
refuse *v.*
region *n.*
regular *adj.*
regularly *adv.*
relation *n.*
relationship *n.*
relax *v.*
relaxed *adj.*
release *v.*
relevant *adj.*
relief *n.*
religion *n.*
religious *adj.*
rely *v.*
remain *v.*
remark *n.*
remember *v.*
remind *v.*
remove *v.*
rent *n., v.*
repair *v., n.*

repeat *v.*
replace *v.*
reply *n., v.*
report *v., n.*
reporter *n.*
represent *v.*
request *n., v.*
require *v.*
rescue *v.*
research *n., v.*
reservation *n.*
respect *n., v.*
responsibility *n.*
responsible *adj.*
rest *n., v.*
restaurant *n.*
result *n., v.*
return *v., n.*
rice *n.*
rich *adj.*
rid *v.*: get rid of
ride *v., n.*
right *adj., adv., n.*
ring *n., v.*
rise *n., v.*
risk *n., v.*
river *n.*
road *n.*
rob *v.*
rock *n.*
role *n.*
roll *n., v.*
romantic *adj.*
roof *n.*
room *n.*
root *n.*
rope *n.*
rough *adj.*
round *adj.*
route *n.*
row *n.*
royal *adj.*
rub *v.*
rubber *n.*
rude *adj.*
   rudely *adv.*
ruin *v.*
rule *n., v.*
run *v., n.*
rush *v.*

S
sad *adj.*
sadness *n.*
safe *adj.*
safely *adv.*
safety *n.*
sail *v.*
salad *n.*

sale *n.*
salt *n.*
same *adj., pron.*
sand *n.*
satisfaction *n.*
satisfied *adj.*
sauce *n.*
save *v.*
say *v.*
scale *n.*
scare *v.*
scared *adj.*
scary *adj.*
schedule *n.*
school *n.*
science *n.*
scientific *adj.*
scientist *n.*
scissors *n.*
score *n., v.*
scratch *v., n.*
screen *n.*
search *n., v.*
season *n.*
seat *n.*
second *adj., adv., n.*
secret *adj., n.*
secretary *n.*
secretly *adv.*
section *n.*
see *v.*
seed *n.*
seem *v.*
sell *v.*
send *v.*
senior *adj.*
sense *n.*
sensible *adj.*
sensitive *adj.*
sentence n.
separate *adj., v.*
separately *adv.*
series *n.*
serious *adj.*
serve *v.*
service *n.*
set *n., v.*
settle *v.*
several *adj., pron.*
sew *v.*
sex *n.*
sexual *adj.*
shade *n.*
shadow *n.*
shake *v.*
shame *n.*
shape *n., v.*
   shaped *adj.*
share *v., n.*

sharp *adj.*
she *pron.*
sheep *n.*
sheet *n.*
shelf *n.*
shell *n.*
shine *v.*
shiny *adj.*
ship *n.*
shirt *n.*
shock *n., v.*
shoe *n.*
shoot *v.*
shop *v.*
shopping *n.*
short *adj.*
shot *n.*
should *modal v.*
shoulder *n.*
shout *v., n.*
show *v., n.*
shower *n.*
shut *v.*
shy *adj.*
sick *adj.*
side *n.*
sight *n.*
sign *n., v.*
signal *n.*
silence *n.*
silly *adj.*
silver *n., adj.*
similar *adj.*
simple *adj.*
since *prep., conj., adv.*
sing *v.*
singer *n.*
single *adj.*
sink *v.*
sir *n.*
sister *n.*
sit *v.*
situation *n.*
size *n.*
skill *n.*
skin *n.*
skirt *n.*
sky *n.*
sleep *v., n.*
sleeve *n.*
slice *n.*
slide *v.*
slightly *adv.*
slip *v.*
slow *adj.*
slowly *adv.*
small *adj.*
smell *v., n.*
smile *v., n.*

smoke *n., v.*
smooth *adj.*
   smoothly *adv.*
snake *n.*
snow *n., v.*
so *adv., conj.*
soap *n.*
social *adj.*
society *n.*
sock *n.*
soft *adj.*
soil *n.*
soldier *n.*
solid *adj., n.*
solution *n.*
solve *v.*
some *adj., pron.*
somebody *pron.*
somehow *adv.*
someone *pron.*
something *pron.*
sometimes *adv.*
somewhere *adv.*
son *n.*
song *n.*
soon *adv.*
   as soon as
sore *adj.*
sorry *adj.*
sort *n., v.*
sound *n., v.*
soup *n.*
south *n., adj., adv.*
southern *adj.*
space *n.*
speak *v.*
speaker *n.*
special *adj.*
speech *n.*
speed *n.*
spell *v.*
spend *v.*
spice *n.*
spider *n.*
spirit *n.*
spoil *v.*
spoon *n.*
sport *n.*
spot *n.*
spread *v.*
spring *n.*
square *adj., n.*
stage *n.*
stair *n.*
stamp *n.*
stand *v., n.*
standard *n., adj.*
star *n.*
stare *v.*